An Amish Woman

An Amish woman's dresses are modest and simple, made of solid-colored fabrics in colors from only half of the color wheel (red-violet to, and including, green). Th
es close in front with either straight pins or snaps and are usually covered by bl
aprons.

Baking

From Amish kitchens come a smorgasbord of tasty treats. Baking is both a necessity for feeding large families and also an opportunity for sharing with others. Bake sales are a common means of raising money for someone in need.

Washing

Clothes are laundered in a wringer washer and hung out to dry on a line that often stretches from the house to the barn. Washing the family's clothes is a big job, but with Mamm and the girls working together on a clear, sunny day, the job is soon done.

Courting

Taking a girl home after a Sunday evening singing is often the start of courting for many Amish couples. Weddings take place in the home of the bride during the month of November, after the field work is done and before winter weather arrives.

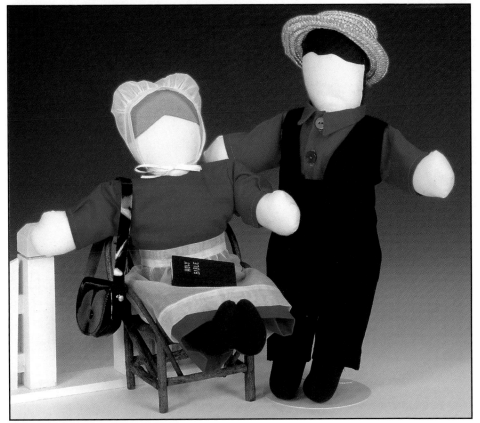

An Amish Girl

A young Amish girl wears simple, modest dresses that button or snap in the back, and a black pinafore apron, until she reaches adolescence. After that, her dresses open in the front and she wears a black half apron.

Raking Leaves

Work is important, and all Amish children are given regular chores around home, whether they live on a farm or not. Working together fosters family closeness, an important value among the Amish.

An Amish Boy

A young Amish boy dresses like his father in solid-colored shirts and long black pants, held up by suspenders.

He gets his first hat at a very young age and wears it daily.

Knitting

Knitting, embroidery, and needlework are hobbies which Amish women reserve for quiet evenings or for when their work is done. Amish girls make and store away many masterfully crafted pillowcases, afghans, and pillows in anticipation of marriage.

Visiting

Grandparents are loved and respected. In many homes, they live in family quarters adjoining the main house. This provides many wonderful opportunities for sharing skills, stories, and wisdom between the generations.

Vegetable Gardening

Gardens are bountiful. They are planted carefully so as to provide for next winter and to produce more than the family needs, so they can sell vegetables at their roadside stand. From the first peas in May through the last pumpkins in October, all ages help with the gardening.

An Amish Man

An Amish man's shirts are made of solid-colored fabrics; his pants are made of black fabric, closed with buttons rather than a zipper.

After marriage, an Amish man begins letting his beard grow, but he does not grow a mustache.

Farming

Although some Amish have left farming for trades such as carpentering, painting, and furniture-making, most prefer farming and the way of life it offers. An appreciation for the land, the opportunity to work together as a family, and to work at home, make farming especially desirable.

Quilting

Girls are taught to sew at a young age, and to enjoy it. For many Amish women, quilting is a satisfying combination of work and pleasure.

Flower-Gardening

Many Amish homes are known for their well-manicured lawns and flower beds. While this responsibility most often falls to the women, the men occasionally help.

Fishing

Work and play cannot be separated, and every Amish boy has a favorite fishing hole. When their chores are finished, the boys hope for another chance at the Big One and perhaps a dip in the creek to cool off.

Amish Doll Patterns

AN AMISH FAMILY AND FRIENDS

Amish Doll Patterns

AN AMISH FAMILY AND FRIENDS

Jan Steffy Mast

Good Books

Intercourse, PA 17534
800/762-7171
www.goodbks.com

Design by Dawn J. Ranck
Photographs by Jonathan Charles

AMISH DOLL PATTERNS: AN AMISH FAMILY AND FRIENDS
© 2001 by Good Books, Intercourse, Pennsylvania 17534
International Standard Book Number: 1-56148-294-3
Library of Congress Catalog Card Number: 99-051553

Library of Congress Cataloging-in-Publication Data
Mast, Jan.
    Amish doll patterns: an Amish family and friends / Jan Steffy Mast.
        p. cm.
    Includes bibliographical references.
    ISBN 1-56148-294-3
    1. Dollmaking. 2. Amish dolls. 3. Coth dolls. 4. Doll clothes--Patterns.
        I. Title.
    TT175.M38 2001
    745.592'21--dc 21   99-051553

Table of Contents

About Amish Doll Patterns . . .

Why do the Amish so fascinate and intrigue onlookers?

As life becomes increasingly complicated and chaotic, as technology crowds every moment and space, the Amish and their choices draw more visitors to their communities. Their "plainness," their "simplicity," hold great appeal.

Amish dolls capture some of that simple charm. Fashioned without faces and dressed modestly, the dolls serve as reminders of the qualities of character often associated with Amish people.

Here for the first time are patterns for Amish dolls that are easy to make and require relatively little time. They are constructed without faces, in keeping with the Amish tradition of humility and their teaching which cautions against making "graven images." The dolls' clothing is authentically styled after that of the Amish of Lancaster County, Pennsylvania.

This easy-to-use book includes complete patterns and detailed instructions for making 22" adult dolls and 15" child dolls. Here, too, are patterns and thorough directions for creating traditional Amish clothing, with all the basic pieces for women and men, girls and boys.

These straightforward patterns give you the unusual opportunity to make and enjoy the treasure of simple Amish beauty. The dolls, singly or as a set, can add a classic touch to the decor of your home. Or they can become a beloved plaything for a child you cherish. (Don't miss the ideas for creating a variety of Amish character dolls on pages 5-7.)

Amish Doll Patterns is your invitation to follow the Amish practice of combining work and pleasure. Invest a bit of time and employ your creativity; you will enjoy the satisfaction of making a family of Amish dolls to love and treasure for many years to come.

— Jan Steffy Mast

You Can Make an Amish Family and Their Friends

The Amish are industrious. They find great satisfaction in their bountiful fields, their carefully handmade crafts, their delicious and hearty meals. These people of the earth are intriguing characters who also find time to tell stories while working and tending their daily chores.

Why not stretch beyond simply making Amish dolls? Develop your figures into characters; give them names and jobs to do. Imagine an Amish family or neighborhood and fill it with personalities.

Twelve Amish character ideas are outlined below. You can enlarge on these by using your imagination and by picking up a few props at your local arts-and-crafts store. (For example, create a grandmother by using gray fabric for the hair on the woman doll. Or add a vest to the man's clothing and he will be dressed for church or going visiting.)

Let the following suggestions stimulate you to make heirlooms for yourself and those you love.

David, Linda Mae, and Lizzie love school.

Annie makes a quilt to sell.

Quilting

Girls are taught to sew at a young age, and to enjoy it. For many Amish women, quilting is a satisfying combination of work and pleasure.

Going to School

Amish children attend one-room schools. They study basic reading, writing, and arithmetic. School functions such as Christmas programs and year-end picnics are popular social events for the whole community.

Dawdi and Mami (Grandpa and Grandma) come for a visit.

Ben fishes after his chores are done.

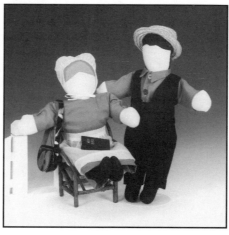

Levi and Rachel will be married in November.

Uncle Amos grows vegetables to sell.

Katie and Mamm (Mom) do the wash.

Visiting

Grandparents are loved and respected. In many homes, they live in family quarters adjoining the main house. This provides many wonderful opportunities for sharing skills, stories, and wisdom between the generations.

Fishing

Work and play cannot be separated, and every Amish boy has a favorite fishing hole. When their chores are finished, the boys hope for another chance at the Big One and perhaps a dip in the creek to cool off.

Courting

Taking a girl home after a Sunday evening singing is often the start of courting for many Amish couples. Weddings take place in the home of the bride during the month of November, after the field work is done and before winter weather arrives.

Vegetable Gardening

Gardens are bountiful. They are planted carefully so as to provide for next winter and to produce more than the family needs, so they can sell vegetables at their roadside stand. From the first peas in May through the last pumpkins in October, all ages help with the gardening.

Washing

Clothes are laundered in a wringer washer and hung out to dry on a line that often stretches from the house to the barn. Washing the family's clothes is a big job, but with Mamm and the girls working together on a clear, sunny day, the job is soon done.

Farming

Although some Amish have left farming for trades such as carpentering, painting, and furniture-making, most prefer farming and the way of life it offers. An appreciation for the land, the opportunity to work together as a family, and to work at home, make farming especially desirable.

Knitting

Knitting, embroidery, and needlework are hobbies which Amish women reserve for quiet evenings or for when their work is done. Amish girls make and store away many masterfully crafted pillowcases, afghans, and pillows in anticipation of marriage.

Flower-Gardening

Many Amish homes are known for their well-manicured lawns and flower beds. While this responsibility most often falls to the women, the men occasionally help.

Raking Leaves

Work is important, and all Amish children are given regular chores around home, whether they live on a farm or not. Working together fosters family closeness, an important value among the Amish.

Baking

From Amish kitchens come a smorgasbord of tasty treats. Baking is both a necessity for feeding large families and also an opportunity for sharing with others. Bake sales are a common means of raising money for someone in need.

Jake wants to grow up to be a farmer.

Mami (Grandma) knits an afghan.

John and Susie grow flowers.

Raking leaves is one of Isaac's chores.

Mary helps Aunt Sadie with baking.

7

Glossary of Terms

— · — · — · — · — · — **Fold**—Place lines designated in this way on fold of fabric.

──────────
- - - - - - - - - - - - -

Seam Allowance—The area between the seam line and the cutting line—1/4″ in width.

◇◇ **Notches**—Used for matching pattern pieces.

──────────
- - - - - - - - - - - - -

Edgestitching—Done on the right side of fabric. Stitch close to seam or finished edge.

Press—Press seams *open* unless otherwise stated.

Gather—Machine-baste designated distance from raw edge using large stitches. Then pull bobbin thread to adjust fabric to its instructed length. Remove gathering threads after sewing seam and securing gathers.

Slipstitch—Hand-stitch, catching a tiny section of fabric so that stitching is invisible.

Staystitch—Machine-stitch 1/4″ from raw edge of fabric to prevent stretching.

Amish Woman Doll and Clothes

An Amish woman's dress is modest and simple, made of a solid-colored fabric in colors from only half of the color wheel (red-violet to, and including, green). The dress is closed in front with either straight pins or snaps and is usually covered by a black apron which is fastened in the back. She wears a black cape for church and other dress-up occasions.

An Amish woman parts her hair in the center and twists it into a tidy bun low on the back of her head. She places a white head covering over her hair, tying the covering strings for church and letting them fly loose for everyday. When she goes away, she puts on a black bonnet, black stockings, and black, laced shoes.

Woman's Body

Supplies Needed

½ yd. flesh-colored fabric or muslin

⅛ yd. black fabric for boots

¼ yd. brown fabric for hair (fabric for hair color can vary according to your preference)

6-8 oz. polyester stuffing

thread (cream, black, and brown)

Cutting Instructions

Arm (A) (pattern on page 41) — Cut 4 of muslin.

Boot (B) (pattern on page 43) — Cut 4 of black fabric.

Leg (C) (pattern on page 43) — Cut 4 of muslin.

Hair Front (D) (pattern on page 45) — Cut 2 of brown fabric on fold.

Body Top/Body Bottom (E) and (E-1) (patterns on pages 39-41) — Tape pieces together as indicated. Cut 2 of muslin on fold.

Hair Back (F) (pattern on page 45) — Cut 1 of brown fabric.

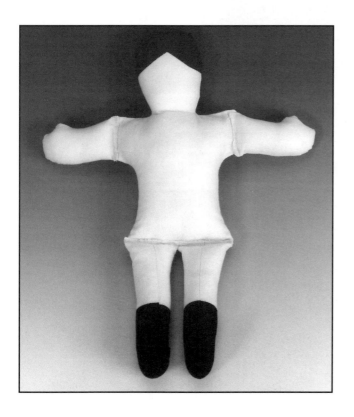

Assembly Instructions

1. Press under ¼" on notched edge of each arm (A) piece.

2. Sew two arm sections together, leaving pressed notched edge open. Clip curves and turn arm right side out. Repeat for second arm. Stuff each arm firmly with polyester stuffing to within ¾" of arm opening.

3. Sew arm openings closed at pressed edges. Sew again ¼" from first seam.

4. Using black thread, sew one boot (B) piece to one leg (C) piece, with right sides together and notches matching. Press seam toward boot. Repeat for all other leg and boot pieces.

5. Press under ¼" on top unnotched edge of each leg piece.

6. With right sides together and using black thread, sew two leg/boot sections together around boot part only. Clip to dot at curve of foot and clip other curves of boot. Repeat for second leg/boot sections.

7. Switch to cream thread and finish sewing sides of leg sections for each leg, leaving pressed, unnotched edge open. Turn legs right side out. Stuff each leg and boot firmly with polyester stuffing to within ¾" of leg opening.

8. Pin leg opening closed with front and back seams centered on top of each other. Sew leg openings closed at pressed edge. Sew again ¼" from first seam.

9. Open each hair front (D) piece and lay with right sides together. Sew along single-notched curved edge with thread the color of the hair fabric. Clip curves, especially at hair-part line. Turn right side out and press.

10. Position hair front, matching double notches to head of one body (E) piece. Baste in place.

11. Press under ¼" along bottom edge of hair back (F). Edgestitch close to fold. Position hair back, matching double notches to head of other body piece. Baste in place.

12. With right sides together, sew body sections together, leaving the bottom edge of the body open for turning right side out.

13. Clip to dot at neck and shoulder joint and clip all other curves. Turn body right side out.

14. With the thumb positioned up, overlap an arm with a shoulder section on body by ¼". Pin in place. Sew through all thicknesses to attach arm to body. Repeat for other arm.

15. Press ¼" seam allowance under at body bottom.

16. Stuff head and upper torso firmly with polyester stuffing to within ¾" of body bottom.

17. Matching pressed edges of bottom edge of body, sew opening closed.

18. With the toes pointing forward, overlap a leg with the bottom edge of the body by ¼". Pin in place. Repeat for other leg. Sew through all thicknesses to attach legs to body.

Woman's Dress

Supplies Needed

½ yd. purple fabric (color of fabric can vary according to your preference)

two small snaps or velcro strip

thread (same color as fabric chosen)

Cutting Instructions

Bodice Back (A) (pattern on page 63) — Cut 2 of purple fabric on fold.

Bodice Front (B) (pattern on page 61) — Cut 2 of purple fabric on fold.

Sleeve (C) (pattern on page 55) — Cut 2 of purple fabric.

Dress (D), (D-1), (D-2), and (D-3) (patterns on pages 57-63) — Tape pieces together as indicated. Cut 1 of purple fabric on fold.

Assembly Instructions

1. Lay unfolded bodice back (A) pieces with right sides together and stitch pieces together at unnotched curve of neck. Clip curve and turn right side out. Press.

2. With right sides together on *one* bodice front (B) piece, sew unnotched curve of neck. Clip curve and turn right side out. Press. Repeat for other bodice front piece.

3. Open bodice back at shoulder seam and lay one opened bodice front, right sides together, against it. Match notches and sew seam. Repeat for other shoulder seam. Press seams open before turning right side out, so that shoulder seams lay flat on bodice.

4. Fold tucks in sleeve (C) hem as indicated on pattern. Press and then tack in place. Hem bottom edge of both sleeves by pressing up ¼", turning up again ¼", and then edgestitching close to the first fold.

5. With right sides together, pin one sleeve to armhole curve of bodice. (Notch on sleeve should be centered on shoulder seam.) Stitch in place. Repeat for second sleeve.

6. With right sides together sew side and sleeve seam on each side of bodice. Turn right side out for completed bodice. Overlap right bodice front over left bodice front by ½". Machine-tack in place at raw edge of bodice bottom.

7. Transfer waistline tuck markings from skirt (D) pattern to fabric. Fold waistline pleats in the direction of the arrows, matching one line to the next and creating six pleats. Pin each pleat in place to hold. Press pleats in place at least as far down as directed on pattern.

8. With right sides together, sew center back seam of dress bottom. Press seam open.

9. With right sides together and raw edges even, fit bodice inside dress bottom, centering overlap of bodice front between center pleats of bottom. Adjust a pleat if necessary to make it fit. Sew in place.

10. Hem bottom edge of skirt by pressing up ¼", turning up again 1½", and then edgestitching close to first fold.

11. Sew snaps or velcro to bodice front (as indicated on pattern) to close dress.

Woman's Apron

Supplies Needed

⅓ yd. black fabric

2 small snaps or velcro strip

black thread

Cutting Instructions

Apron (A) and (A-1) (patterns on page 65-67) — Tape pieces together as indicated. Cut 1 of black fabric on fold.

Apron Waistband (B) (pattern on page 69) — Cut 1 of black fabric on fold.

Assembly Instructions

1. Hem sides of apron (A) by pressing under ¼", turning under again ¼", and then edgestitching close to first fold.

2. Hem bottom of apron by pressing up ¼", turning up again 1½", and then edgestitching close to first fold.

3. Sew loose gathering stitch ¼" from top edge of apron.

4. Press under ¼" on unnotched long edge of apron waistband (B).

5. With right sides together, adjust gathering stitches to make apron edges fit between notches of *un*pressed edge of waistband. Adjust to fit and then sew in place. Press seam allowance toward waistband.

6. Press up ¼" seam allowance of waistband extension section (between apron and end of band). Fold waistband in half lengthwise, with right sides together, and sew ends together. Clip seam allowance at corners of extension and turn waistband right side out.

7. Press waistband in place so that open edge just covers the seam that joined the waistband to the apron. Edgestitch entire length of waistband to finish.

8. Fit apron on doll, overlapping extensions until there is a 1"-1¼" gap at apron back. Note overlap amount, remove apron, and sew snaps or velcro in place to fasten apron extensions.

Woman's Cape

Supplies Needed

¼ yd. black fabric

4 small snaps or velcro strip

black thread

Cutting Instructions

Cape Front (A) (pattern on page 71) — Cut 4 of black fabric.

Cape Back (B) (pattern on page 71) — Cut 2 of black fabric.

Assembly Instructions

1. With right sides together and notches matching sew two cape front (A) pieces to one cape back (B) at shoulder seam. Repeat for other front and back pieces. Press seams open.

2. Pin cape pieces with right sides together. Sew around all edges, except at bottom of cape back as indicated on pattern.

   Clip corners and curve at neck. Turn piece right side out through opening. Push out points and press.

3. Turn opening edge up ¼" to inside and handsew closed to finish.

4. Overlap cape right front over left front ½" and sew two snaps or velcro in place in order to close cape.

5. Fit cape on doll, tucking bottom points under front and back of apron waistband. Note overlap amount, remove, and sew snaps or velcro in place to attach cape to apron.

Woman's Covering

Supplies Needed

¼ yd. white organdy (sheer, stiff fabric)

½ yd. white ⅛"-¼"-wide ribbon

white thread

Cutting Instructions

Covering (A) (pattern on page 73) — Cut 1 of white organdy on fold.

Covering Brim (B) (pattern on page 73) — Cut 1 of white organdy on fold.

Assembly Instructions

1. With covering piece (A) folded in half as it was when cut out, topstitch ⅛" from folded edge as indicated on pattern. Open covering and press tiny pleat to one side.

2. Hem bottom edge of covering by pressing up ¼", turning up again ¼", and then edgestitching close to the first fold.

3. Sew a medium to long gathering stitch ¼" from outside edge of covering. Sew a second gathering line ⅛" from first, toward covering outer edge, as shown on pattern.

4. Hem two short edges and one long edge of covering brim (B) by pressing up ¼", turning up again ¼", and then edgestitching close to the first fold.

5. Pin covering brim to covering with right sides together and raw edges even. Adjust gathering stitches to fit. Gathers should be fullest at top of covering to create sweetheart curve when turned right side out. Sew covering to brim.

6. Trim seam to ⅛", and then turn brim right side out.

7. Cut two 7" lengths of white ribbon. Machine-tack each ribbon in place at front bottom corners of covering brim, as indicated on pattern.

8. Fit covering on doll, shaping sweetheart curves and fullness at top of covering.

Woman's Bonnet

Supplies Needed

¼ yd. black fabric

¼ yd. black heavyweight fabric

2″ x 12″ piece of pressboard or cardboard

½ yd. black ⅛″-¼″-wide ribbon, cording, or shoelace

black thread

Cutting Instructions

Bonnet Brim (A) (pattern on page 79) — Cut 1 of black fabric on fold.

Bonnet Back (B) (pattern on page 75) — Cut 1 of black fabric. Cut 1 of black heavyweight fabric.

Bonnet Flap (C) (pattern on page 77) — Cut 1 of black fabric on fold.

Assembly Instructions

1. Cut a 2″ x 12″ piece of thin but sturdy and flexible pressboard or cardboard for the brim stiffening.

2. Fold brim (A) piece in half along fold line and place over brim stiffener. Topstitch five lines through all thicknesses as shown on the pattern.

3. Lay lighter weight bonnet back (B) on top of heavyweight fabric bonnet back. Fold tucks along bottom edge as indicated on pattern. Stitch along bottom edge, through all thicknesses, to hold in place.

4. Pin tucks in place around outer edge of bonnet back. Hold brim against tucks to check fit. If necessary, adjust or re-space tucks to fit length of brim. When brim fits satisfactorily, remove brim and sew tucks through all thicknesses.

5. With right sides together and raw edges even, pin brim in place. Then sew through all thicknesses. Flip brim out.

6. Fold bonnet flap (C) in half lengthwise with right sides together. Stitch ends and turn right side out. Press.

7. Fold bonnet flap tucks as indicated on pattern. Stitch along raw edge to hold tucks in place.

8. Pin flap to bottom edge of bonnet and brim, matching front edges and bonnet back tucks with flap tucks. Sew through all thicknesses.

9. Cut two 7″ lengths of black ribbon, cording, or shoelace for bonnet ties. Pin in place, ¼″ in from front of brim at dot, as indicated on pattern. Machine-tack in place.

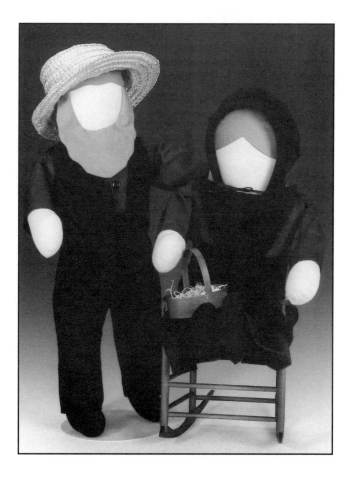

Amish Man Doll and Clothes

An Amish man's shirts are made of solid-colored fabrics. They are basic in style with a turnover collar and buttons up the front. Pants are made of black fabric, closed with buttons rather than a zipper, and are held up with suspenders which cross in an X in the back.

A man wears a simple black vest for church services, other outings, and in cooler weather.

An Amish man gets his hair cut at home, usually by his wife. The typical style is to cut the hair off straight in the back with bangs in the front. After marriage, an Amish man begins letting his beard grow, but he does not grow a mustache.

A hat is an integral part of his daily dress. For church and special occasions, he wears a black hat, but around home and at work, he is more likely to wear a straw hat.

Man's Body

Supplies Needed

½ yd. flesh-colored fabric or muslin

⅛ yd. black fabric for boots

¼ yd. brown fabric for hair and beard (fabric for hair and beard color can vary according to your preference)

6-8 oz. polyester stuffing

thread (cream, black, and brown)

straw hat

Cutting Instructions

Arm (A) (pattern on page 41) — Cut 4 of muslin.

Boot (B) (pattern on page 43) — Cut 4 of black fabric.

Leg (C) (pattern on page 43) — Cut 4 of muslin.

Beard (D) (pattern on page 47) — Cut 2 of brown fabric.

Body Top/Body Bottom (E) and (E-1) (patterns on pages 39-41) — Tape pieces together as indicated. Cut 2 of muslin on fold.

Hair Back (F) (pattern on page 45) — Cut 1 of brown fabric.

Hair Front (G) (pattern on page 47) — Cut 2 of brown fabric.

Assembly Instructions

1. Press under ¼" on notched edge of each arm (A) piece.

2. Sew two arm sections together, leaving pressed notched edge open. Clip curves and turn arm right side out. Repeat for second arm. Stuff each arm firmly with polyester stuffing to within ¾" of arm opening.

3. Sew arm openings closed at pressed edge. Sew again ¼" from first seam.

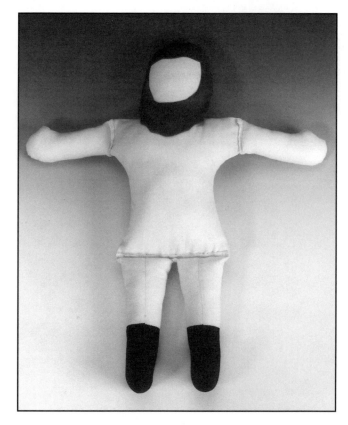

4. Using black thread, sew one boot (B) piece to one leg (C) piece with right sides together and notches matching. Press seam toward boot. Repeat for all other leg and boot pieces.

5. Press under ¼" on top unnotched edge of each leg piece.

6. With right sides together and using black thread, sew two leg/boot sections together around boot part only. Clip to dot at curve of foot and clip other curves of boot. Repeat for second leg/boot sections.

7. Switch to cream thread and finish sewing sides of leg sections for each leg, leaving pressed, unnotched edge open. Turn legs right side out. Stuff each leg and boot firmly with polyester stuffing to within ¾" of leg opening.

8. Pin leg opening closed with front and back seams centered on top of each other. Sew leg openings closed at pressed edge. Sew again ¼" from first seam.

9. With right sides together, sew beard (D) pieces together along curvy edge without dots. Clip curves and turn right side out. Press.

10. Staystitch ¼" from raw edges on remaining sides with dots. Clip to staystitched seam along curve of beard. Press these clipped sections along staystitched seam to back side of beard.

11. Position beard on one body (E) piece, matching pressed/staystitched edge with curve indicated on pattern. Lift beard outer edges carefully to get at clipped sections. Pin these clipped sections to hold beard in place.

12. Sew beard to face underneath along staystitched seam. (Clipped sections and raw edges should not be visible when beard is lying flat against face).

13. With right sides together, sew hair front (G) pieces together along unnotched curved edges. (Use thread the color of hair fabric). Clip curves, turn right side out, and press.

14. Position hair front, matching double notches and overlapping raw edges of beard ends, to head. Baste in place.

15. Press under ¼" along bottom edge of hair back (F). Edgestitch close to fold. Position hair back, matching double notches to head of other body piece. Baste in place.

16. Fold beard edges in toward center of face, away from arm and face edges. Tack or pin in place, so the beard doesn't get caught in remaining seams.

17. With right sides together, sew body sections together, leaving the bottom edge of the body open for turning right side out.

18. Clip to dot at neck and shoulder joint, and clip all other curves. Turn body right side out. Untack beard and, if necessary, press so it lies flat.

19. With the thumb positioned up, overlap an arm with a shoulder section on body by ¼". Pin in place. Sew through all thicknesses to attach arm to body. Repeat for other arm.

20. Press ¼" seam allowance under at body bottom.

21. Stuff head and upper torso firmly with polyester stuffing to within ¾" of body bottom.

22. Matching pressed edges of bottom edge of body, sew opening closed.

23. With the toes pointing forward, overlap a leg with the bottom edge of the body by ¼". Pin in place. Repeat for other leg. Sew through all thicknesses to attach legs to body.

19

Man's Shirt

Supplies Needed

¼ yd. blue fabric (color of fabric can vary according to your preference)

3 buttons, ¼"-⅜" in diameter

thread (same color as fabric chosen)

Cutting Instructions

Shirt Front (A) (pattern on page 81) — Cut 2 of blue fabric.

Shirt Back (B) (pattern on page 83) — Cut 1 of blue fabric on fold.

Sleeve (C) (pattern on page 85) — Cut 2 of blue fabric.

Collar (D) (pattern on page 83) — Cut 2 of blue fabric.

Assembly Instructions

1. With right sides together, sew shirt front pieces (A) to shirt back (B) at shoulder seams. Press seams open.

2. Hem bottom edge of each sleeve by pressing up ¼", turning up again ¼", and then edgestitching close to first fold.

3. With right sides together, pin sleeve (C) to sleeve opening on shirt front and back. Notch on sleeve should match shoulder seam. Stitch in place. Repeat for other sleeve.

4. With right sides together, sew collar (D) pieces together along three unnotched sides. Trim seam, especially at collar points. Turn right side out and press.

5. Pin collar to shirt, matching notches and having raw edges even. Sew in place.

6. Turn front edge of each shirt front under ¼" and press. Edgestitch close to fold.

7. Fold shirt front on fold line with right sides together. Sew from fold to hemmed edge at collar. Trim seam and turn right side out.

8. Press along fold line to form facing for buttons and button holes.

9. With right sides together, sew side seam and sleeve seam in one continuous seam. Repeat for other side/sleeve. Clip curves at underarms.

10. Hem bottom edge of shirt by pressing up ¼", turning up again ¼", and then edgestitching close to first fold.

11. Sew three buttons and make three buttonholes on shirt front as indicated on pattern.

Man's Pants

Supplies Needed

¼ yd. black fabric

¾ yd. ½"-wide black elastic for suspenders

2 black buttons, ½" in diameter

black thread

Cutting Instructions

Pants Front and Back (A) and (A-1) (patterns on
page 87-89) — Tape pieces together as indicated.
Cut 4 of black fabric.

Assembly Instructions

1. With right sides together and notches matching,
   sew two pants (A) pieces together along notched
   edges to form pants front. Repeat and sew other
   two pieces together along notched edges to form
   pants back. Press seams open.

2. Press under ¼" along top edge of pants front
   and pants back. Edgestitch close to fold on each
   piece. Fold this finished edge to inside, pressing
   on fold line.

3. Sew darts in pants back through all thicknesses,
   as indicated on pattern. Press darts toward center.

4. With right sides together, sew pants front to
   pants back through crotch and inseam in one
   continuous seam. Press seam open.

5. Hem pant legs by pressing each one up ¼",
   turning up again ¼", and edgestitching close to
   first fold.

6. With right sides together and waistband turned
   up, sew side seams. Turn pants right side out
   and turn waistband to inside.

7. Cut two 10¾" lengths of ½"-wide black elastic.
   Machine-tack elastic suspenders to pants front,
   overlapping fold line of pants by ¼" on inside at
   dots, as indicated on pattern.

8. Cross suspenders to form an X and machine-
   tack to pants back at an angle, overlapping fold
   line of pants by ¼" on inside at dots, as indicated on pattern.

9. Handsew two black buttons to front of pants at
   each suspender, covering machine-tacking.

Man's Vest

Supplies Needed

¼ yd. black fabric

black thread

Cutting Instructions

Vest Front (A) (pattern on page 89) — Cut 4 of black fabric.

Vest Back (B) (pattern on page 91) — Cut 2 of black fabric on fold.

Assembly Instructions

1. Matching notches, sew two vest fronts (A) to a vest back (B) at shoulder seams. Repeat for other set of fronts and back. Press seams open.

2. With right sides together, pin one front/back vest unit to the other front/back unit. Stitch all seams except side seams, stopping stitching on *fronts* at dots as indicated on pattern.

3. Trim corners and clip curves.

4. Turn vest right side out through one side opening. Press.

5. To finish side seams, bring right sides together. Stitch through three thicknesses, leaving one *front* inner seam allowance free.

6. Fold free seam allowance under ¼". Press stitched seam allowances toward folded seam allowance. Bring folded seam allowance over the stitched seam to cover all raw edges. Slipstitch in place.

Amish Girl Doll and Clothes

A young Amish girl wears her hair fashioned like her mother's, in a simple bun with a center part. For church and other formal occasions she covers her head with a white covering, and for going away in cooler weather, she wears a bonnet. This bonnet is made of a solid-colored fabric, such as blue or purple, until she reaches age 10. After that, she wears a black bonnet, also like her mother's.

Her dresses, simple and modest like her mother's, are buttoned or snapped up the back until she reaches adolescence. Then her dresses are made to open up the front. The fabrics, though solid-colored, are often brighter shades of the colors adult women wear.

A young girl wears a black pinafore apron, which opens in the back, until adolescence; thereafter, a black half apron completes her outfit. (She wears a white version of the pinafore apron or half apron for church until she marries. After that, she will wear a black apron for church also.)

Many Amish persons—women, men, and children—go barefoot around home in warm weather. Most put on black stockings and shoes to go away.

Girl's Body

Supplies Needed

¼ yd. flesh-colored fabric or muslin

⅛ yd. black fabric for boots

⅛ yd. brown fabric for hair (fabric for hair color can vary according to your preference)

4-6 oz. polyester stuffing

thread (cream, black, and brown)

Cutting Instructions

Arm (A) (pattern on page 51) — Cut 4 of muslin.

Boot (B) (pattern on page 53) — Cut 4 of black fabric.

Leg (C) (pattern on page 53) — Cut 4 of muslin.

Girl's Hair Front (D) (pattern on page 53) — Cut 2 of brown fabric on fold.

Child's Body (E) and (E-1) (patterns on pages 49-51) — Tape pieces together as indicated. Cut 2 of muslin.

Hair Back (F) (pattern on page 51) — Cut 1 of brown fabric.

Assembly Instructions

1. Press under ¼" on notched edge of each arm (A) piece.

2. Sew two arm sections together, leaving pressed notched edge open. Clip curves and turn arm right side out. Repeat for second arm. Stuff each arm firmly with polyester stuffing to within ¾" of arm opening.

3. Sew arm openings closed at pressed edges. Sew again ¼" from first seam.

4. Using black thread, sew one boot (B) piece to one leg (C) piece, with right sides together and notches matching. Press seam toward boot. Repeat for all other leg and boot pieces.

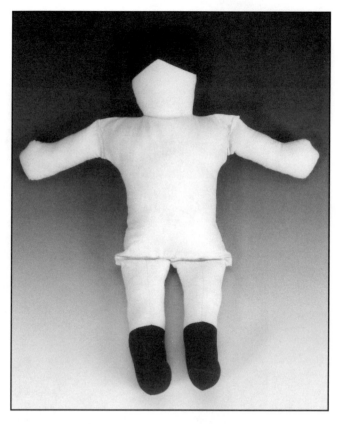

5. Press under ¼" on top unnotched edge of each leg piece.

6. With right sides together and using black thread, sew two leg/boot sections together around boot part only. Clip to dot at curve of foot; clip other curves of boot. Repeat for second leg/boot sections.

7. Switch to cream thread and finish sewing sides of leg sections for each leg, leaving pressed, unnotched edge open. Turn legs right side out. Stuff each leg and boot firmly with polyester stuffing to within ¾" of leg opening.

8. Pin leg opening closed with front and back seams centered on top of each other. Sew leg openings closed at pressed edge. Sew again ¼" from first seam.

9. Open each hair front (D) piece and lay with right sides together. Sew along single-notched, curved edge with thread the color of the hair fabric. Clip curves, especially at hair part-line. Turn right side out and press.

10. Position hair front, matching double notches to head of one body (E) piece. Baste in place.

11. Press under ¼" along bottom edge of hair back (F). Edgestitch close to fold. Position hair back, matching double notches to head of other body piece. Baste in place.

12. With right sides together, sew body sections together, leaving the bottom edge of the body open for turning right side out.

13. Clip to dot at neck and shoulder joint, and clip all other curves. Turn body right side out.

14. With the thumb positioned up, overlap an arm with a shoulder section on body by ¼". Pin in place. Sew through all thicknesses to attach arm to body. Repeat for other arm.

15. Press ¼" seam allowance under at body bottom.

16. Stuff head and upper torso firmly with polyester stuffing to within ¾" of body bottom.

17. Matching pressed edges of bottom edge of body, sew opening closed.

18. With the toes pointing forward, overlap a leg with the bottom edge of the body by ¼". Pin in place. Repeat for other leg. Sew through all thicknesses to attach legs to body.

Girl's Dress

Supplies Needed

⅓ yd. mauve fabric (color of fabric can vary according to your preference)

one small snap or velcro strip

thread (same color as fabric chosen)

Cutting Instructions

Bodice Front (A) (pattern on page 93) — Cut 2 of mauve fabric on fold.

Bodice Back (B) (pattern on page 93) — Cut 2 of mauve fabric on fold.

Sleeve (C) (pattern on page 97) — Cut 2 of mauve fabric.

Dress Bottom (D) and (D-1) (pattern on pages 95-97) — Tape pieces together as indicated. Cut 1 of mauve fabric on fold.

Assembly Instructions

1. Lay unfolded bodice front pieces (A) with right sides together and stitch pieces together at unnotched curve of neck. Clip curve and turn right side out. Press.

2. With right sides together on *one* bodice back (B) piece, sew unnotched curve of neck. Clip curve and turn right side out. Press. Repeat for other bodice back piece.

3. Open one bodice front at shoulder seam and lay other opened bodice front, right sides together, against it. Match notches and sew seam. Repeat for other shoulder seam. Press seams open before turning right side out, so that shoulder seams lie flat on bodice.

4. Fold tucks in sleeve (C) hem as indicated on pattern. Press and then tack in place. Hem bottom edge of both sleeves by pressing up ¼", turning up again ¼", and then edgestitching close to the first fold.

5. With right sides together, pin one sleeve to armhole curve of bodice. (Notch on sleeve should be centered on shoulder seam.) Stitch in place. Repeat for second sleeve.

6. With right sides together sew side and sleeve seam on each side of bodice. Turn right side out for completed bodice.

7. Transfer waistline tuck markings from skirt (D) pattern to fabric. Fold waistline pleats in the direction of the arrows, matching one line to the next to create six pleats. Pin each pleat in place to hold. Press pleats in place at least as far down as directed on pattern.

8. With right sides together pin bodice to skirt, starting ¼" in from each edge of skirt at dots. Adjust a pleat if necessary to make bodice fit. Sew in place.

9. With right sides together, sew skirt back seam together. Tack well where bodice joins skirt. Press seam open.

10. Hem bottom edge of skirt by pressing up ¼", turning up again 1", and then edgestitching close to first fold.

11. Sew a snap or velcro strip to bodice back (as indicated on pattern) to fasten dress.

Girl's Apron

Supplies Needed

¼ yd. black fabric

2 small snaps or velcro strip

black thread

Cutting Instructions

Apron (A) (pattern on page 99) — Cut 1 of black fabric on fold.

Apron Waistband (B) (pattern on page 101) — Cut 1 of black fabric on fold.

Assembly Instructions

1. Hem sides of apron (A) by pressing under ¼", turning under again ¼", and then edgestitching close to first fold.

2. Hem bottom of apron by pressing up ¼", turning up 1", and then edgestitching close to first fold.

3. Sew loose gathering stitch ¼" from top edge of apron.

4. Press under ¼" on unnotched long edge of apron waistband (B).

5. With right sides together, adjust gathering stitches to make apron edges fit between notches of *un*pressed edge of waistband. Adjust to fit and then sew in place. Press seam allowance toward waistband.

6. Press up ¼" seam allowance of waistband extension section (between edge of apron and end of band). Fold waistband in half lengthwise with right sides together and sew ends together. Clip seam allowance at corners of extension and turn waistband right side out.

7. Press waistband in place so that open edge just covers the seam that joined the waistband to the apron. Edgestitch entire length of waistband to finish.

8. Fit apron on doll, overlapping extensions until there is a ½"- ¾" gap at apron back. Note overlap amount, remove apron, and sew snaps or velcro in place to fasten apron extensions.

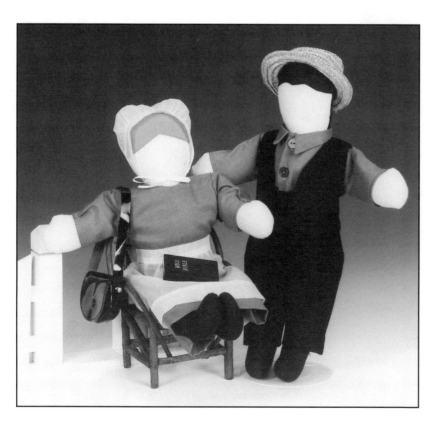

Girl's Pinafore Apron

Supplies Needed

½ yd. black fabric

1 small snap or velcro strip

black thread

Cutting Instructions

Pinafore Apron (A) and (A-1) (patterns on pages 101-103) — Tape pieces together as indicated. Cut 1 of black fabric on fold.

Sleeve Band (B) (pattern on page 101) — Cut 2 of black fabric.

Assembly Instructions

1. With pinafore apron (A) folded as it was cut out, and with wrong sides together, sew ¾" from center fold from neck edge to dot, as indicated on pattern.

2. Press seam flat from neck edge to hem edge to create decorative front pleat. Tack pleat in place by topstitching through all thicknesses at both markings indicated on pattern.

3. Cut along armhole cutline (indicated on pattern) to dot. With right sides together and notches matching, sew shoulder seams to create an armhole opening.

4. Sew notched ends of sleeve band (B) together. Press seam open. Repeat for other sleeve band.

5. Fold sleeve bands in half lengthwise with wrong sides together. Press.

6. Fit sleeve band into armhole opening with right sides together and raw edges even. Sew in place. Repeat for other sleeve band and armhole.

7. Staystitch ¼" from neck edge. Clip curves and press under on staystitched seam. Edgestitch close to pressed edge to finish neckline.

8. Hem back edge of apron by pressing under ¼", turning under again ¼", and edgestitching close to first fold.

9. Hem bottom edge of apron by pressing up ¼", turning up an additional 1¼", and then edgestitching close to first fold.

10. Overlap apron at neckline ½" and sew a snap or velcro strip in place to fasten apron.

Girl's Covering

Supplies Needed

¼ yd. white organdy (sheer, stiff fabric)

⅓ yd. white ⅛"-wide ribbon

white thread

Cutting Instructions

Covering (A) (pattern on page 105) — Cut 1 of white organdy on fold.

Covering Brim (B) (pattern on page 105) — Cut 1 of white organdy on fold.

Assembly Instructions

1. With covering piece (A) folded as it was cut out, topstitch ⅛" from folded edge as indicated on pattern. Open covering and press tiny pleat to one side.

2. Hem bottom edge of covering by pressing up ¼", turning up again ¼", and then edgestitching close to the first fold.

3. Sew a medium to long gathering stitch ¼" from outside edge of covering. Sew a second gathering line ⅛" from first, toward covering outer edge, as shown on pattern.

4. Hem two short edges and one long edge of covering brim (B) by pressing up ¼", turning up again ¼", and then edgestitching close to the first fold.

5. Pin covering brim to covering with right sides together and raw edges even. Adjust gathering stitches to fit. Gathers should be fullest at top of covering to create sweetheart curve when turned right side out. Sew covering to brim.

6. Trim seam to ⅛", and then turn brim right side out.

7. Cut two 6" lengths of white ribbon. Machine-tack each ribbon in place at front bottom corners of covering brim, as indicated on pattern.

8. Fit covering on doll, shaping sweetheart curves and fullness at top of covering.

Girl's Bonnet

Supplies Needed

¼ yd. black or dark fabric

1½" x 8½" piece of pressboard or cardboard

⅓ yd. black ⅛"-¼"-wide ribbon, cording, or shoelace

black or dark thread

Cutting Instructions

Bonnet Brim (A) (pattern on page 109) — Cut 1 of black fabric.

Bonnet Back (B) (pattern on page 107) — Cut 2 of black fabric.

Bonnet Flap (C) (pattern on page 105) — Cut 1 of black fabric on fold.

Assembly Instructions

1. Cut a 1½" x 8½" piece of thin but sturdy and flexible pressboard or cardboard for the brim stiffening.

2. Fold brim (A) piece in half along fold line and place over brim stiffener. Topstitch three lines through all thicknesses as shown on the pattern.

3. Lay bonnet back pieces (B) on top of each other. Fold tucks along bottom edge as indicated on pattern. Stitch along bottom edge through all thicknesses to hold in place.

4. Pin tucks in place around outer edge of bonnet back. Hold brim against tucks to check fit. If necessary, adjust or re-space tuck to fit length of brim. When brim fits satisfactorily, remove brim and sew tucks through all thicknesses.

5. With right sides together and raw edges even, pin brim in place. Then sew through all thicknesses. Flip brim out.

6. Fold bonnet flap (C) in half lengthwise with right sides together. Stitch ends and turn right side out. Press.

7. Fold bonnet flap tucks as indicated on pattern. Stitch along raw edge to hold tucks in place.

8. Pin flap to bottom edge of bonnet and brim, matching front edges and bonnet back tucks with flap tucks. Sew through all thicknesses.

9. Cut two 6" lengths of black ribbon, cording, or shoelace for bonnet ties. Pin in place, ¼" in from front of brim at dot, as indicated on pattern. Machine-tack in place.

Amish Boy Doll and Clothes

A young Amish boy dresses like his father in a solid-colored shirt which buttons up the front and has a turned collar at the neck. He wears long black pants year-round, held up by suspenders crossed in the back, instead of a belt.

His hairstyle is like all the other Amish men and boys in his community—cut off straight in the back and worn in bangs in the front. He gets his first hat at a very young age and wears it daily. His everyday hat is made of straw and his going-away hat is made of black felt.

A black vest, black shoes, and stockings complete his outfit for church and other outings.

Boy's Body

Supplies Needed

¼ yd. flesh-colored fabric or muslin

⅛ yd. black fabric for boots

⅛ yd. brown fabric for hair (fabric for hair color can vary according to your preference)

4-6 oz. polyester stuffing

thread (cream, black, and brown)

straw hat

Cutting Instructions

Arm (A) (pattern on page 51) — Cut 4 of muslin.

Boot (B) (pattern on page 53) — Cut 4 of black fabric.

Leg (C) (pattern on page 53) — Cut 4 of muslin.

Hair Front (D) (pattern on page 53) — Cut 2 of brown fabric.

Body Top/Body Bottom (E) and (E-1) (patterns on pages 49-51) — Tape pieces together as indicated. Cut 2 of muslin.

Hair Back (F) (pattern on page 51) — Cut 1 of brown fabric.

Assembly Instructions

1. Press under ¼" on notched edge of each arm (A) piece.

2. Sew two arm sections together, leaving pressed notched edge open. Clip curves and turn arm right side out. Repeat for second arm. Stuff each arm firmly with polyester stuffing to within ¾" of arm opening.

3. Sew arm openings closed at pressed edges. Sew again ¼" from first seam.

4. Using black thread, sew one boot (B) piece to one leg (C) piece, with right sides together and notches matching. Press seam toward boot. Repeat for all other leg and boot pieces.

5. Press under ¼" on top unnotched edge of each leg piece.

6. With right sides together and using black thread, sew two leg/boot sections together around boot part only. Clip to dot at curve of foot and clip other curves of boot. Repeat for second leg/boot sections.

7. Switch to cream thread and finish sewing sides of leg sections for each leg, leaving pressed, unnotched edge open. Turn legs right side out. Stuff each leg and boot firmly with polyester stuffing to within ¾" of leg opening.

8. Pin leg opening closed with front and back seams centered on top of each other. Sew leg openings closed at pressed edges. Sew again ¼" from first seam.

9. With right sides together, sew hair front (D) pieces together along unnotched curved edges. (Use thread the color of hair fabric). Clip curves, turn right side out and press.

10. Position hair front, matching double notches to body (E). Baste in place.

11. Press under ¼" along bottom edge of hair back (F). Edgestitch close to fold. Position hair back, matching double notches to head of other body piece. Baste in place.

12. With right sides together, sew body sections together, leaving the bottom edge of the body open for turning right side out.

13. Clip to dot at neck and shoulder joint and clip all other curves. Turn body right side out.

14. With the thumb positioned up, overlap an arm with a shoulder section on body by ¼". Pin in place. Sew through all thicknesses to attach arm to body. Repeat for other arm.

15. Press ¼" seam allowance under at body bottom.

16. Stuff head and upper torso firmly with polyester stuffing to within ¾" of body bottom.

17. Matching pressed edges of bottom edge of body, sew opening closed.

18. With the toes pointing forward, overlap a leg with the bottom edge of the body by ¼". Pin in place. Repeat for other leg. Sew through all thicknesses to attach legs to body.

Boy's Shirt

Supplies Needed

¼ yd. teal fabric (color of fabric can vary according to your preference)

3 buttons, ¼"-⅜" in diameter

thread (same color as fabric chosen)

Cutting Instructions

Shirt Front (A) (pattern on page 111) — Cut 2 of teal fabric.

Shirt Back (B) (pattern on page 113) — Cut 1 of teal fabric on fold.

Sleeve (C) (pattern on page 113) — Cut 2 of teal fabric.

Collar (D) (pattern on page 111) — Cut 2 of teal fabric.

Assembly Instructions

1. With right sides together, sew shirt front pieces (A) to shirt back (B) at shoulder seams. Press seams open.

2. Hem bottom edge of each sleeve by pressing up ¼", turning up again ¼", and then edgestitching close to first fold.

3. With right sides together, pin sleeve (C) to sleeve opening on shirt front and back. Notch on sleeve should match shoulder seam. Stitch in place. Repeat for other sleeve.

4. With right sides together, sew collar (D) pieces together along three unnotched sides. Trim seam, especially at collar points. Turn right side out and press.

5. Pin collar to shirt, matching notches and having raw edges even. Sew in place.

6. Turn front edge of each shirt front under ¼" and press. Edgestitch close to fold.

7. Fold shirt front on fold line with right sides together. Sew from fold to hemmed edge at collar. Trim seam and turn right side out.

8. Press along fold line to form facing for buttons and button holes.

9. With right sides together, sew side seam and sleeve seam in one continuous seam. Repeat for other side/sleeve. Clip curves at underarms.

10. Hem bottom edge of shirt by pressing up ¼", turning up again ¼", and then edgestitching close to first fold.

11. Sew three buttons and make three buttonholes on shirt front as indicated on pattern.

Boy's Pants

Supplies Needed

¼ yd. black fabric

½ yd. ¼"-wide black elastic for suspenders

2 buttons, ¼"-⅜" in diameter

black thread

Cutting Instructions

Pants Front and Back (A) (pattern on page 115) —
Cut 4 of black fabric.

Assembly Instructions

1. With right sides together and notches matching, sew two pants (A) pieces together along notched edges to form pants front. Repeat and sew other two pieces together along notched edges to form pants back. Press seams open.

2. Press under ¼" along top edge of pants front and pants back. Edgestitch close to fold on each piece. Fold this finished edge to inside, pressing on fold line.

3. Sew darts in pants back through all thicknesses as indicated on pattern. Press darts toward center.

4. With right sides together sew pants front to pants back through crotch and inseam in one continuous seam. Press seam open.

5. Hem pant legs by pressing each one up ¼", turning up again ¼", and edgestitching close to first fold.

6. With right sides together and waistband turned up, sew side seams. Turn pants right side out and turn waistband to inside.

7. Cut two 7¾" lengths of ¼"-wide black elastic. Machine-tack elastic suspenders to pants front, overlapping fold line of pants by ¼" on inside at dots, as indicated on pattern.

8. Cross suspenders to form an X and machine-tack to pants back at an angle, overlapping fold line of pants by ¼" on inside at dots, as indicated on pattern.

9. Handsew two black buttons to front of pants at each suspender, covering machine-tacking.

Boy's Vest

Supplies Needed

¼ yd. black fabric

black thread

Cutting Instructions

Vest Front (A) (pattern on page 117) — Cut 4 of black fabric.

Vest Back (B) (pattern on page 117) — Cut 2 of black fabric on fold.

Assembly Instructions

1. Matching notches, sew two vest fronts (A) to a vest back (B) at shoulder seams. Repeat for other set of fronts and back. Press seams open.

2. With right sides together, pin one front/back vest unit to the other front/back unit. Stitch all seams except side seams, stopping stitching on *fronts* at dots as indicated on pattern.

3. Trim corners and clip curves.

4. Turn vest right side out through one side opening. Press.

5. To finish side seams, bring right sides together. Stitch through three thicknesses, leaving one *front* inner seam allowance free.

6. Fold free seam allowance under ¼". Press stitched seam allowances toward folded seam allowance. Bring folded seam allowance over the stitched seam to cover all raw edges. Slipstitch in place.

Pattern Templates
for Figures and Clothing

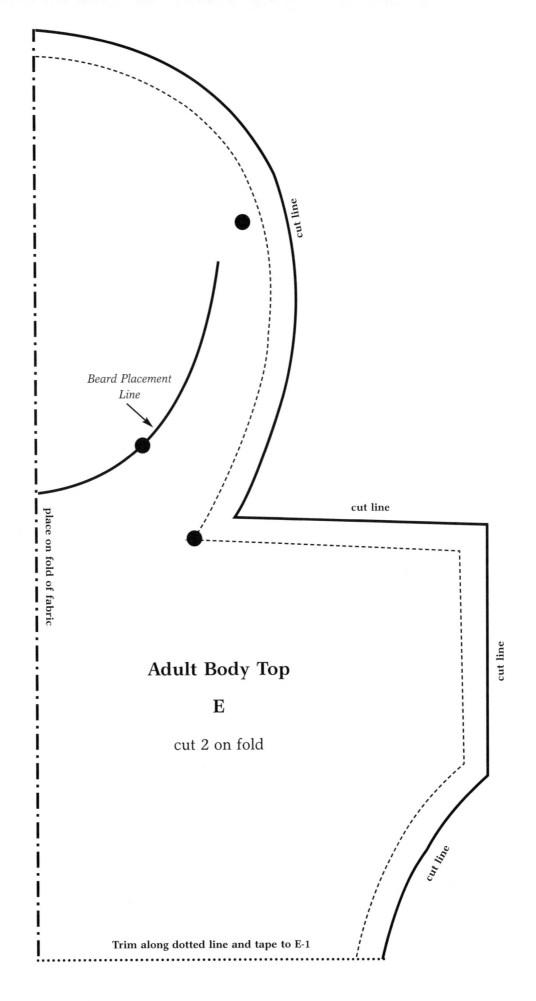

cut line

cut line

cut line

cut line

Beard Placement Line

place on fold of fabric

Adult Body Top

E

cut 2 on fold

Trim along dotted line and tape to E-1

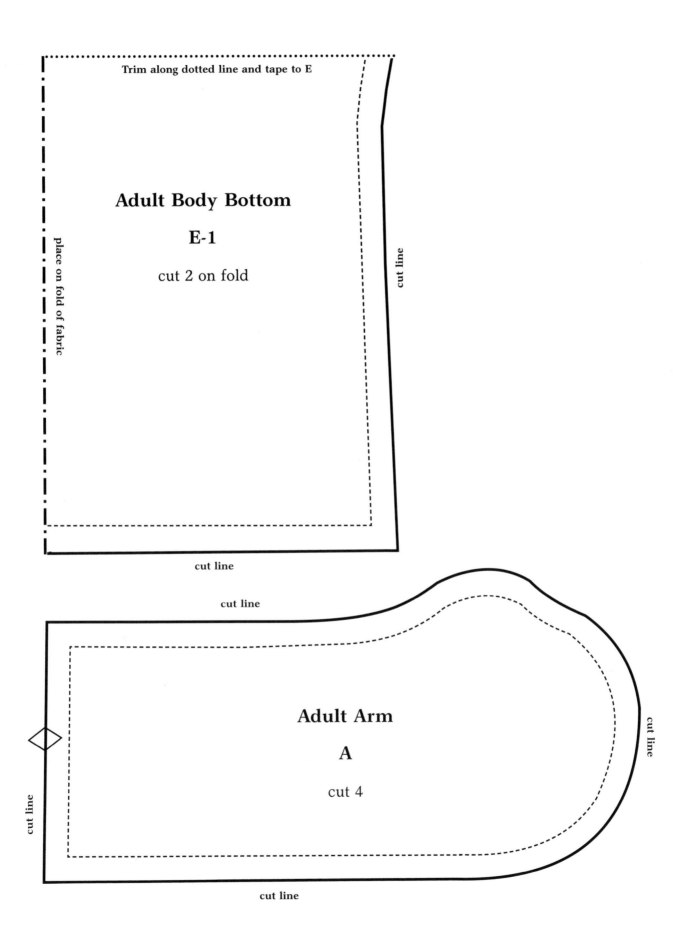

Trim along dotted line and tape to E

place on fold of fabric

Adult Body Bottom

E-1

cut 2 on fold

cut line

cut line

cut line

Adult Arm

A

cut 4

cut line

cut line

cut line

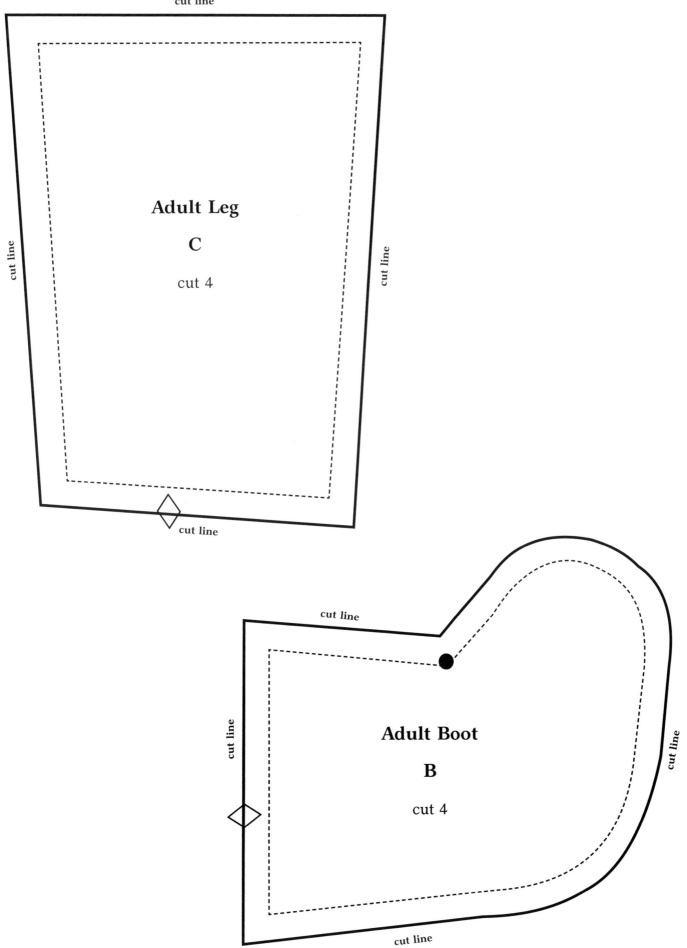

Adult Leg

C

cut 4

cut line

cut line

cut line

cut line

Adult Boot

B

cut 4

cut line

cut line

cut line

cut line

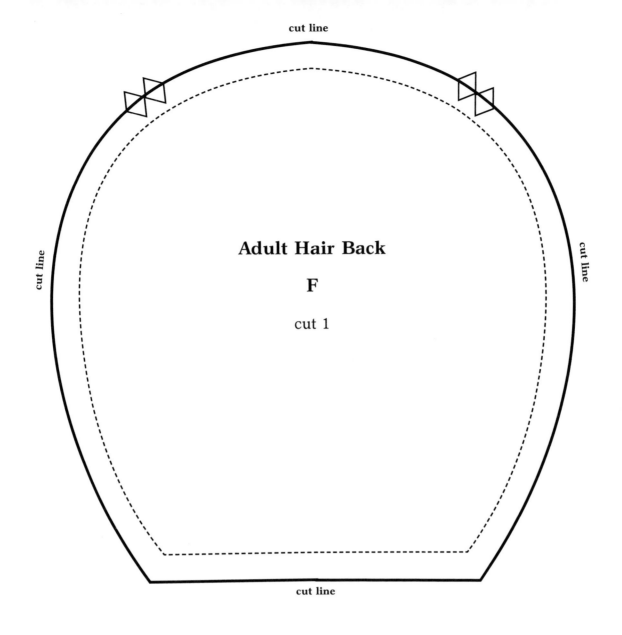

Adult Hair Back

F

cut 1

cut line

cut line

cut line

cut line

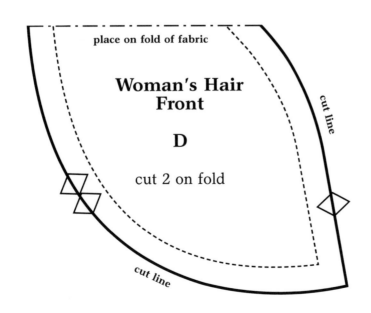

place on fold of fabric

Woman's Hair Front

D

cut 2 on fold

cut line

cut line

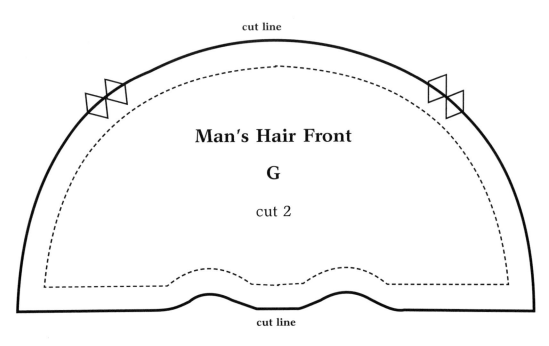

Man's Hair Front

G

cut 2

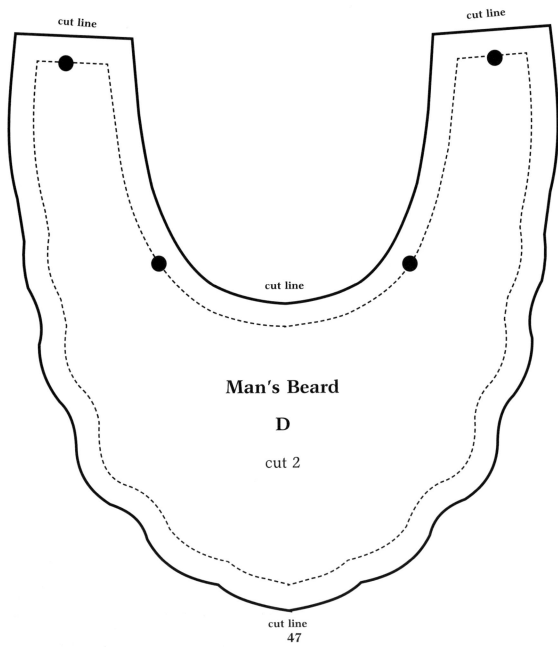

Man's Beard

D

cut 2

47

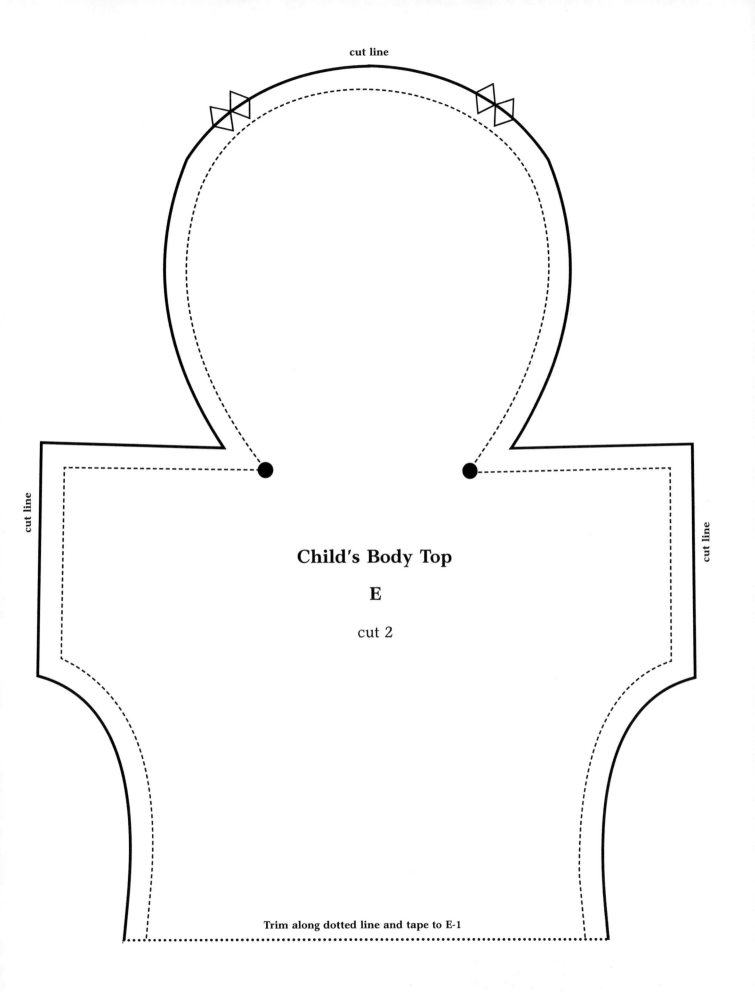

cut line

Child's Body Top

E

cut 2

cut line

cut line

Trim along dotted line and tape to E-1

49

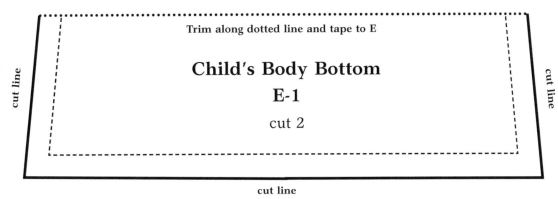

Trim along dotted line and tape to E

Child's Body Bottom
E-1
cut 2

cut line

cut line

cut line

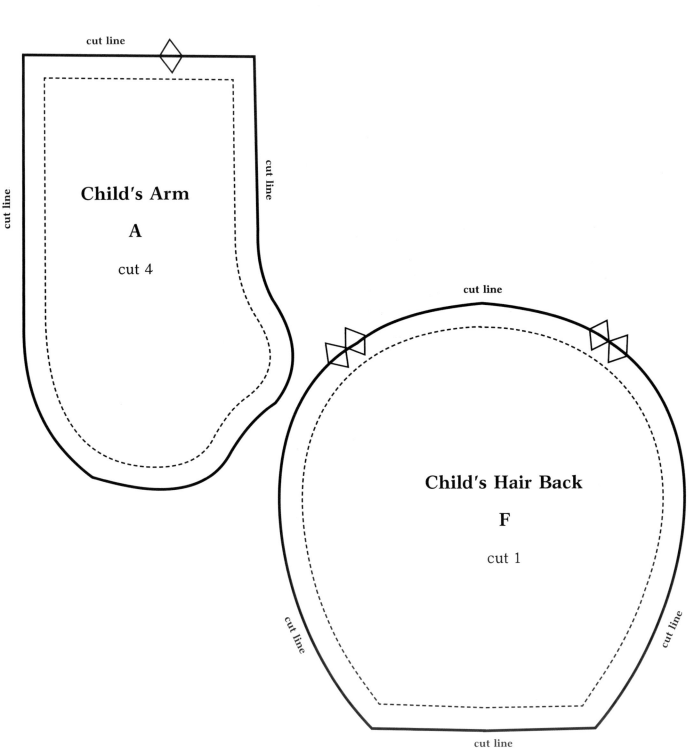

cut line

Child's Arm

A

cut 4

cut line

cut line

cut line

Child's Hair Back

F

cut 1

cut line

cut line

cut line

51

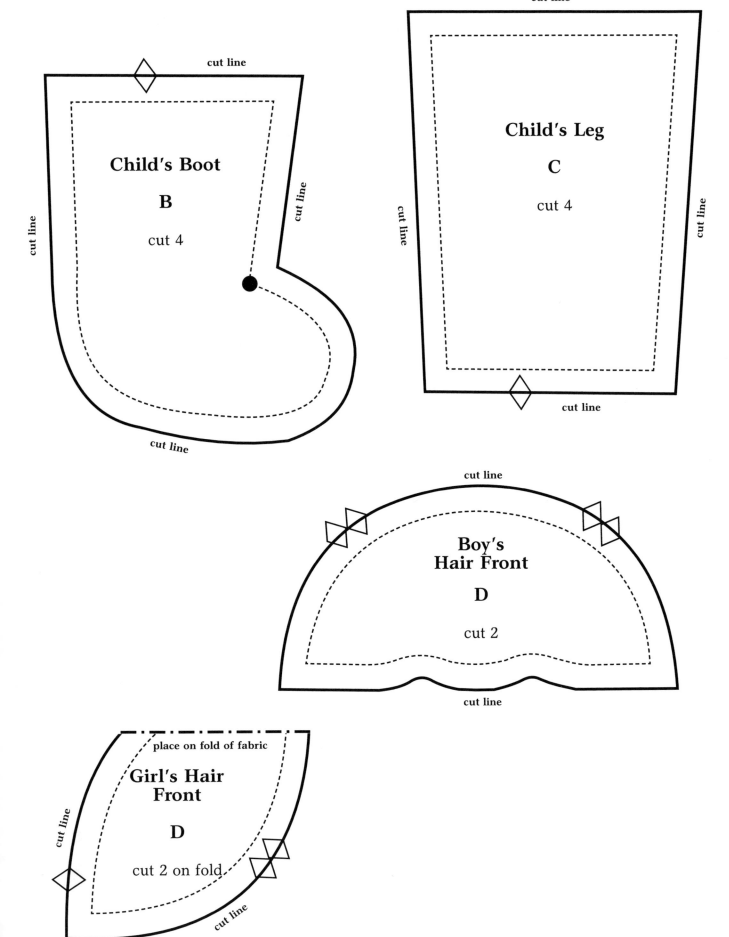

Child's Boot

B

cut 4

cut line

cut line

cut line

cut line

Child's Leg

C

cut 4

cut line

cut line

cut line

cut line

Boy's Hair Front

D

cut 2

cut line

cut line

Girl's Hair Front

D

cut 2 on fold

place on fold of fabric

cut line

cut line

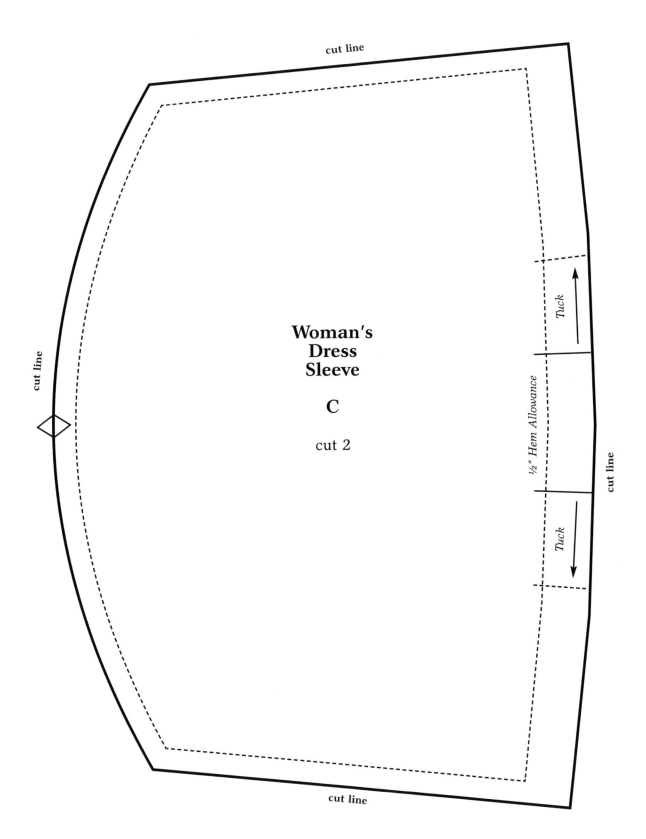

cut line

cut line

cut line

cut line

**Woman's
Dress
Sleeve**

C

cut 2

Tuck

½" *Hem Allowance*

Tuck

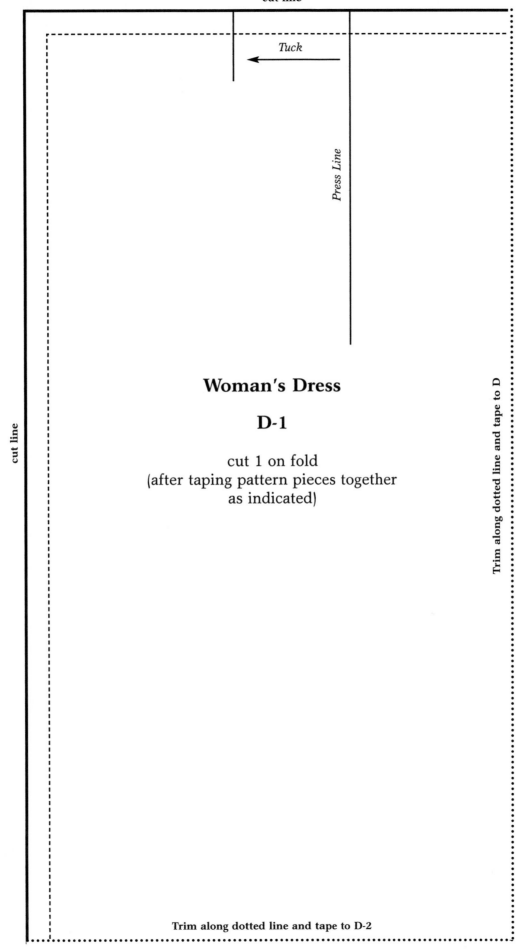

cut line

Tuck

Press Line

Woman's Dress

D-1

cut 1 on fold
(after taping pattern pieces together
as indicated)

Trim along dotted line and tape to D

cut line

Trim along dotted line and tape to D-2

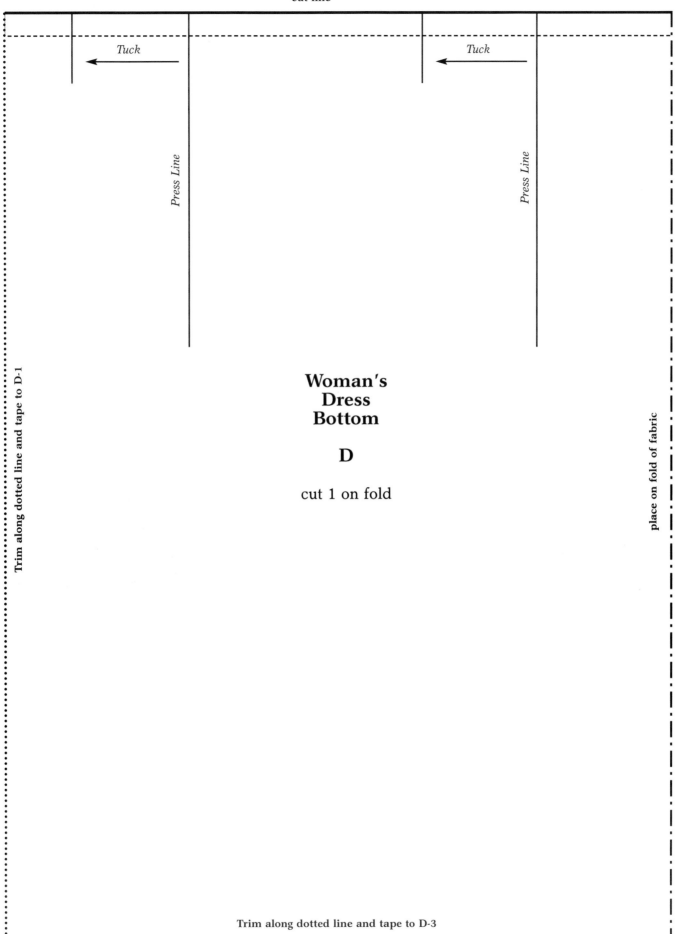

cut line

Tuck

Tuck

Press Line

Press Line

Trim along dotted line and tape to D-1

place on fold of fabric

Woman's Dress Bottom

D

cut 1 on fold

Trim along dotted line and tape to D-3

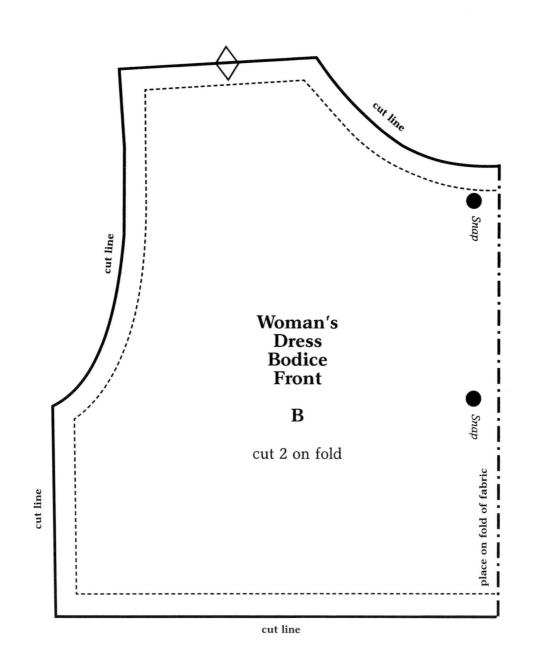

Trim along dotted line and tape to D-2

Trim along dotted line and tape to D

1½" Hem Allowance

Woman's Dress

D-3

cut 1 on fold

place on fold of fabric

cut line

cut line

cut line

cut line

Woman's Dress Bodice Front

B

cut 2 on fold

Snap

Snap

place on fold of fabric

cut line

61

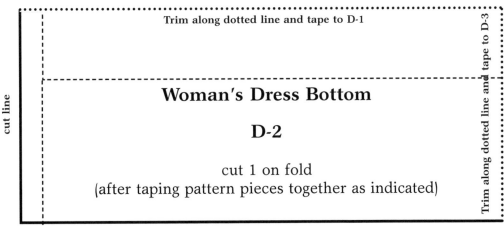

Trim along dotted line and tape to D-1

cut line

Woman's Dress Bottom

D-2

cut 1 on fold
(after taping pattern pieces together as indicated)

Trim along dotted line and tape to D-3

cut line

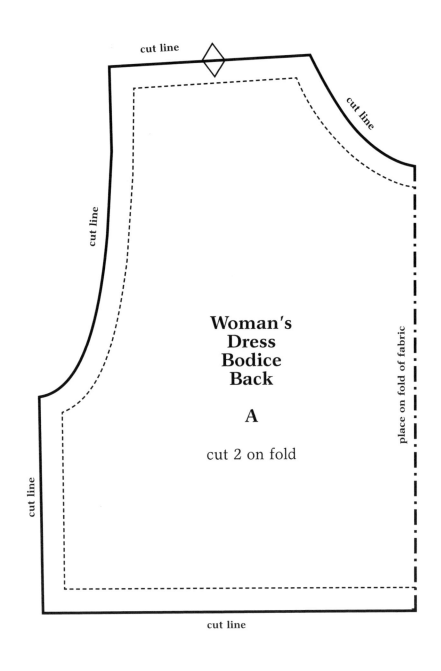

cut line

cut line

cut line

cut line

Woman's Dress Bodice Back

A

cut 2 on fold

place on fold of fabric

cut line

cut line

cut line

Trim along dotted line and tape to A-1

Woman's Apron

A

cut 1 on fold

place on fold of fabric

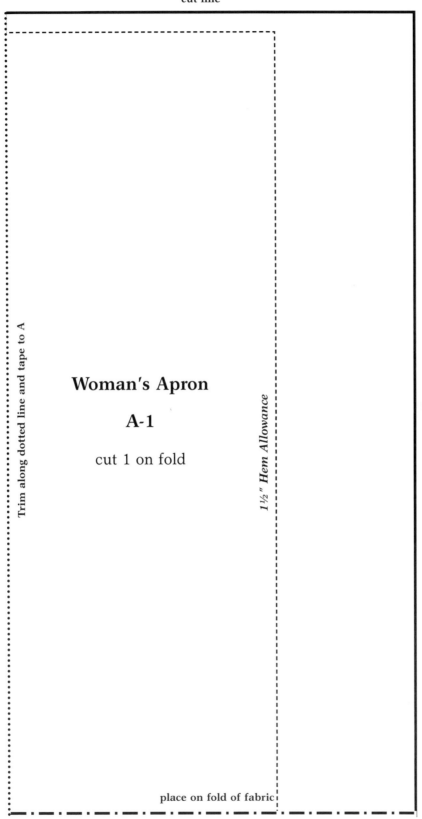

cut line

cut line

Trim along dotted line and tape to A

Woman's Apron

A-1

cut 1 on fold

1½" Hem Allowance

place on fold of fabric

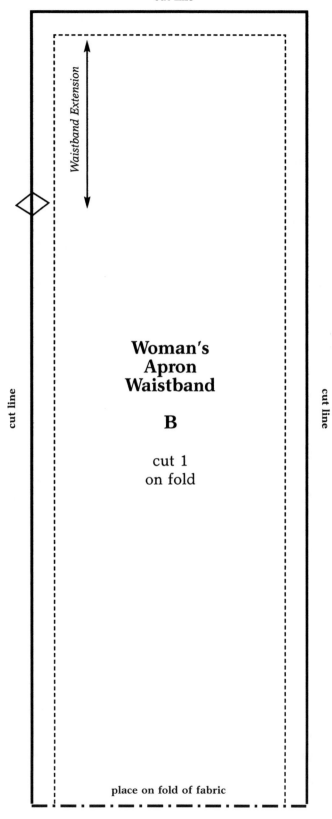

cut line

cut line

cut line

Waistband Extension

**Woman's
Apron
Waistband**

B

cut 1
on fold

place on fold of fabric

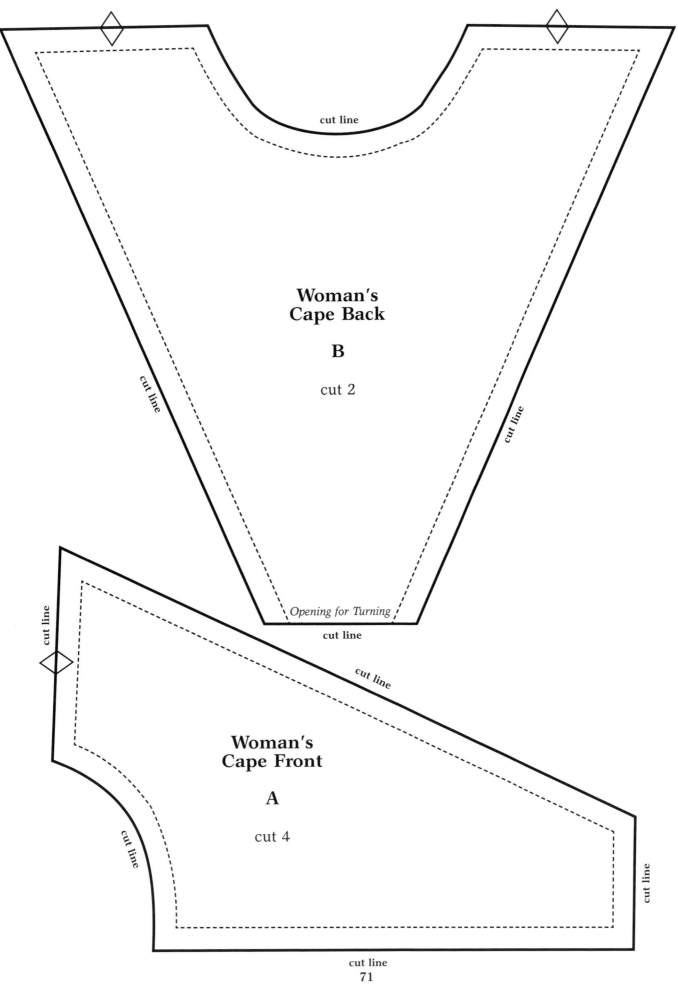

cut line

Woman's
Cape Back

B

cut 2

cut line

cut line

Opening for Turning

cut line

cut line

cut line

cut line

Woman's
Cape Front

A

cut 4

cut line

cut line

cut line
71

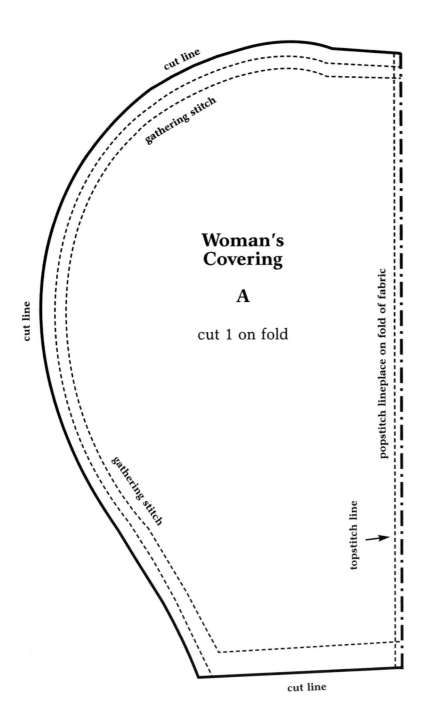

Woman's Covering

A

cut 1 on fold

cut line

cut line

gathering stitch

gathering stitch

popstitch lineplace on fold of fabric

topstitch line

cut line

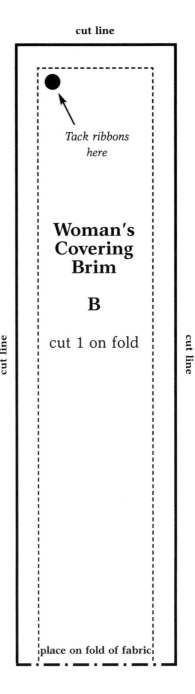

cut line

Tack ribbons here

Woman's Covering Brim

B

cut 1 on fold

cut line

cut line

place on fold of fabric

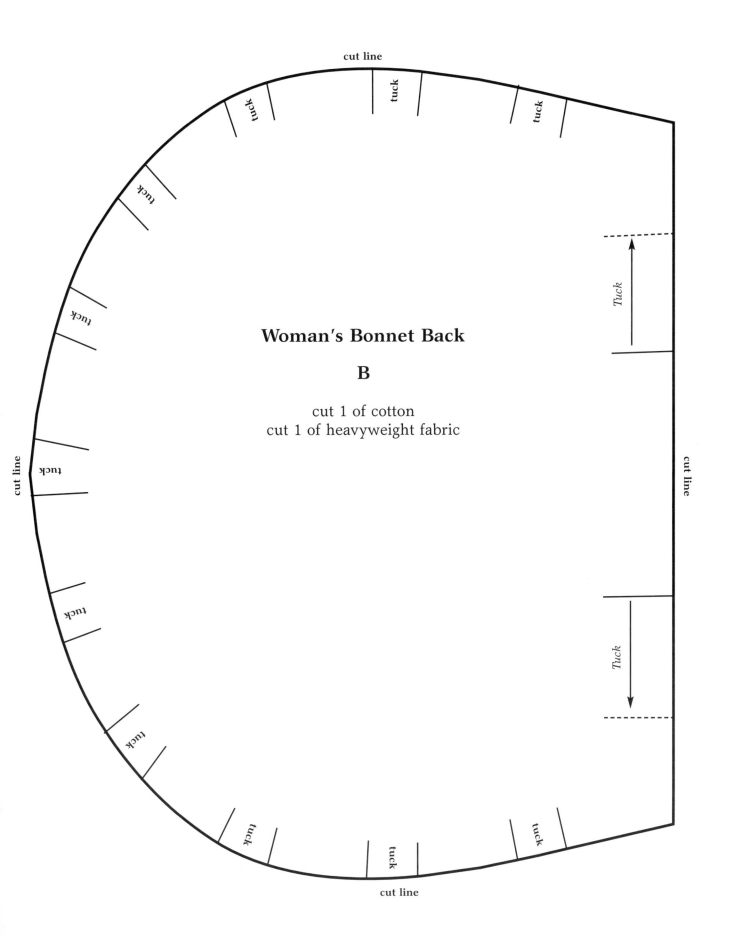

cut line

tuck

tuck

tuck

tuck

tuck

tuck

Tuck

Woman's Bonnet Back

B

cut 1 of cotton
cut 1 of heavyweight fabric

cut line

Tuck

tuck

tuck

tuck

tuck

tuck

cut line

cut line

75

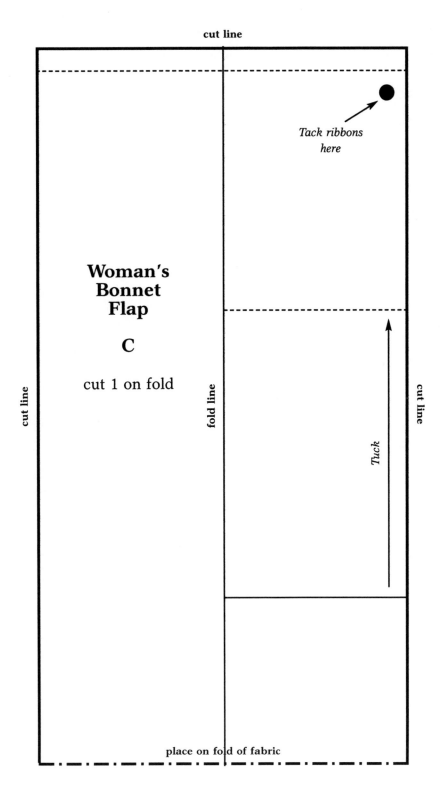

cut line

Tack ribbons here

Woman's Bonnet Flap

C

cut 1 on fold

cut line

fold line

cut line

Tuck

place on fold of fabric

cut line

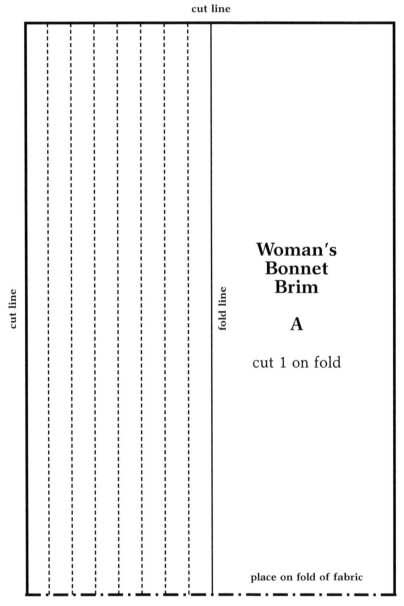

cut line

fold line

Woman's Bonnet Brim

A

cut 1 on fold

cut line

place on fold of fabric

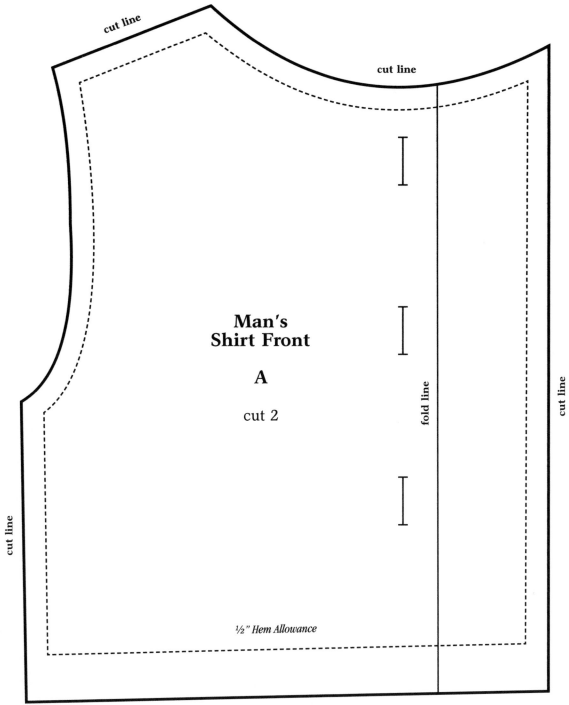

cut line

cut line

cut line

cut line

cut line

**Man's
Shirt Front**

A

cut 2

fold line

½" Hem Allowance

81

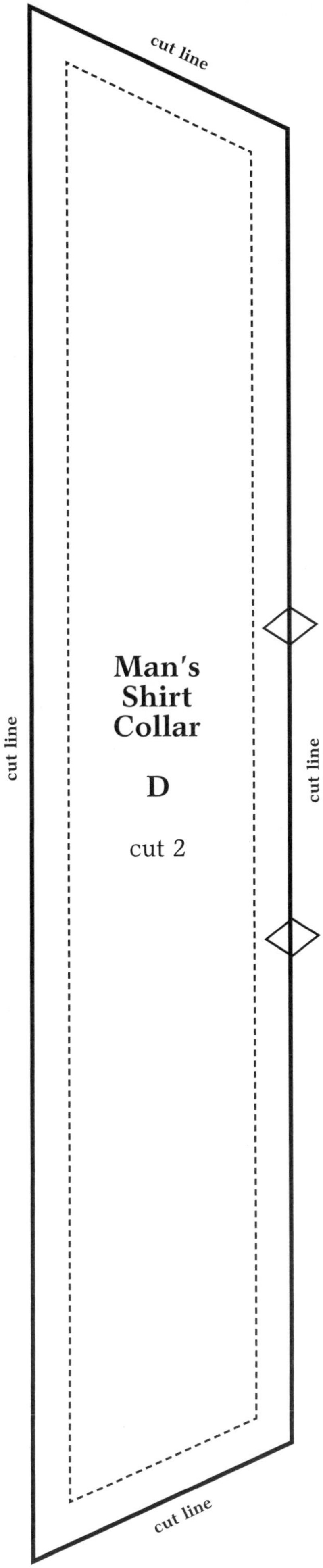

cut line

**Man's
Shirt
Collar**

D

cut 2

cut line

cut line

cut line

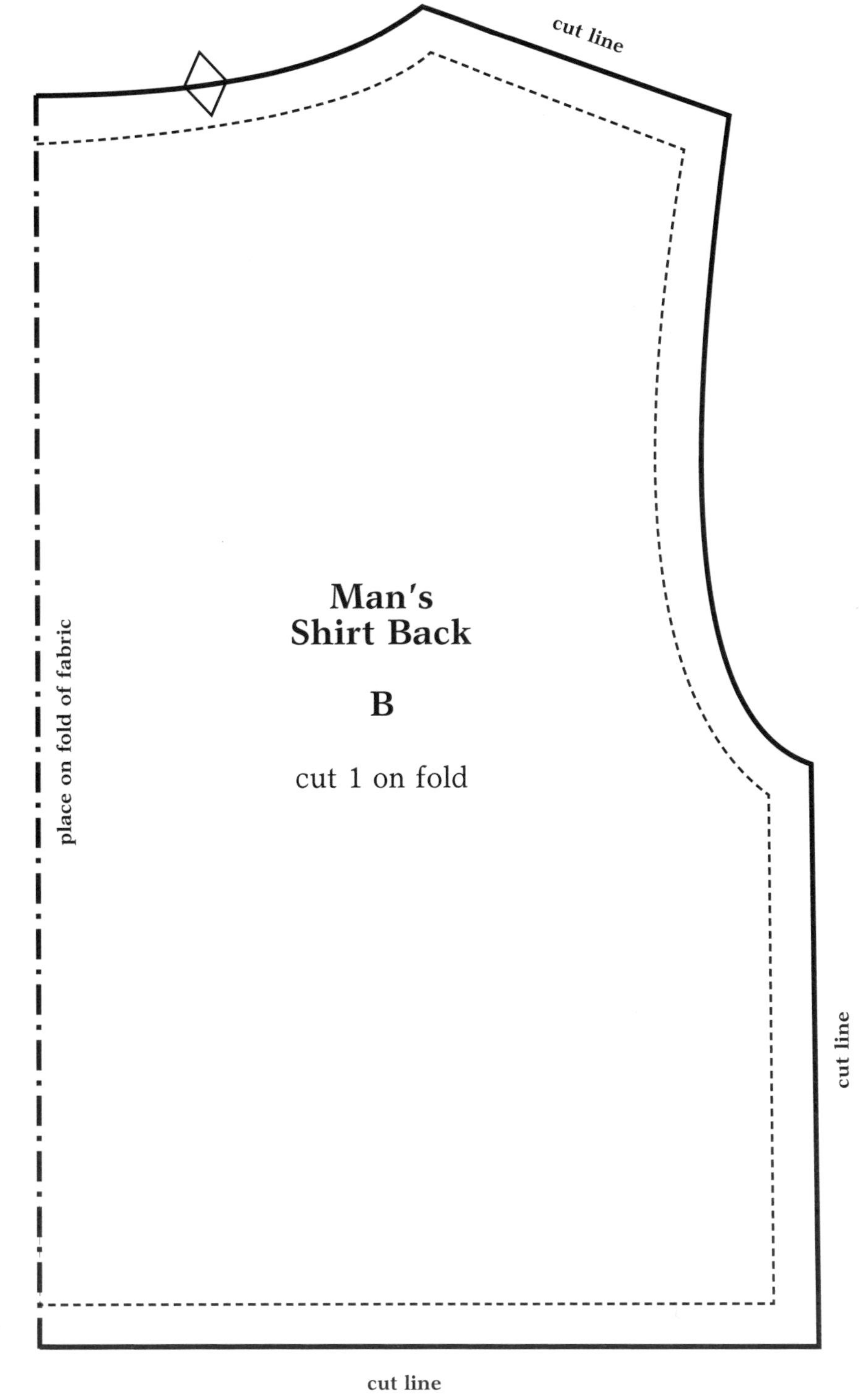

cut line

place on fold of fabric

**Man's
Shirt Back**

B

cut 1 on fold

cut line

cut line

83

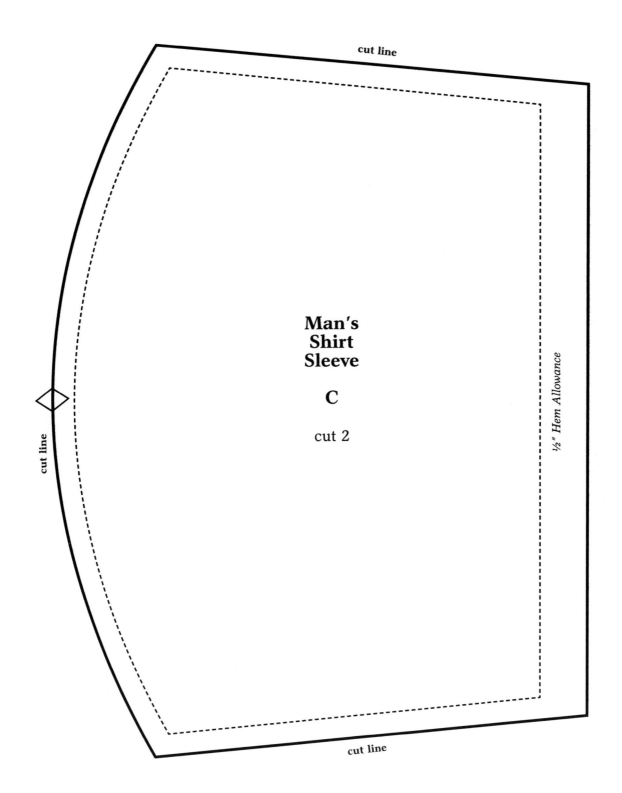

cut line

Man's
Shirt
Sleeve

C

cut 2

½" Hem Allowance

cut line

cut line

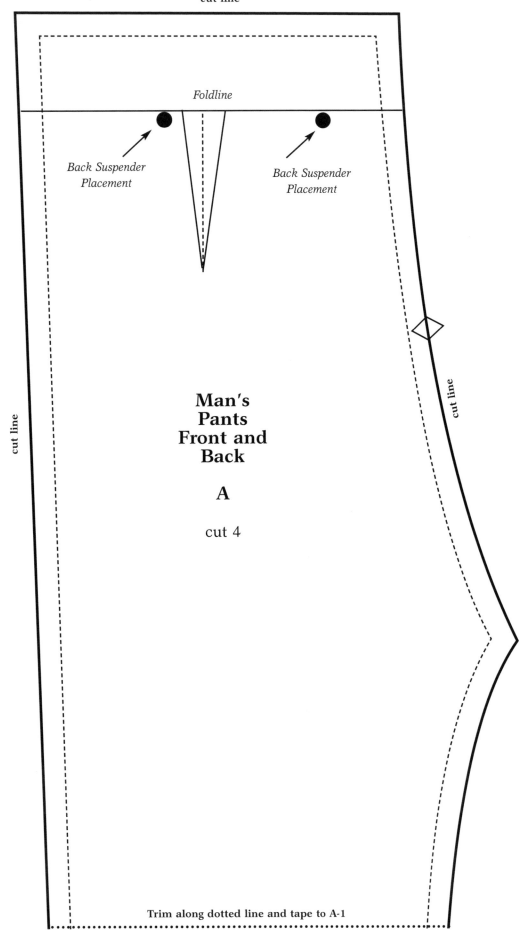

cut line

Foldline

Back Suspender
Placement

Back Suspender
Placement

cut line

cut line

**Man's
Pants
Front and
Back**

A

cut 4

Trim along dotted line and tape to A-1

87

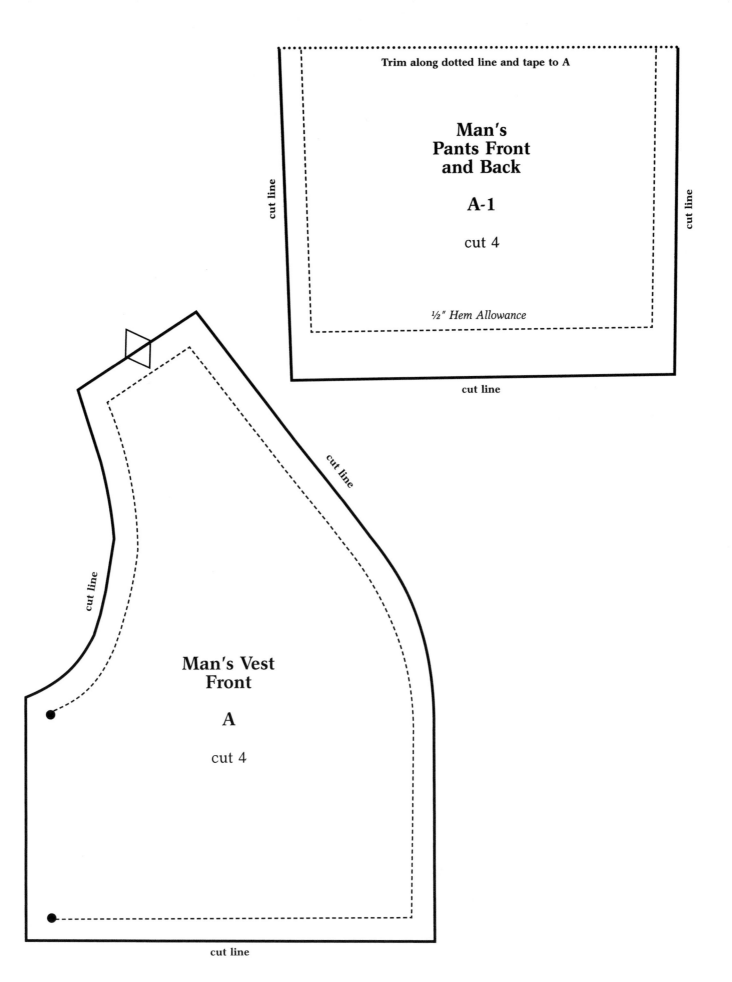

Trim along dotted line and tape to A

**Man's
Pants Front
and Back**

A-1

cut 4

½" Hem Allowance

cut line

cut line

cut line

cut line

cut line

**Man's Vest
Front**

A

cut 4

cut line

89

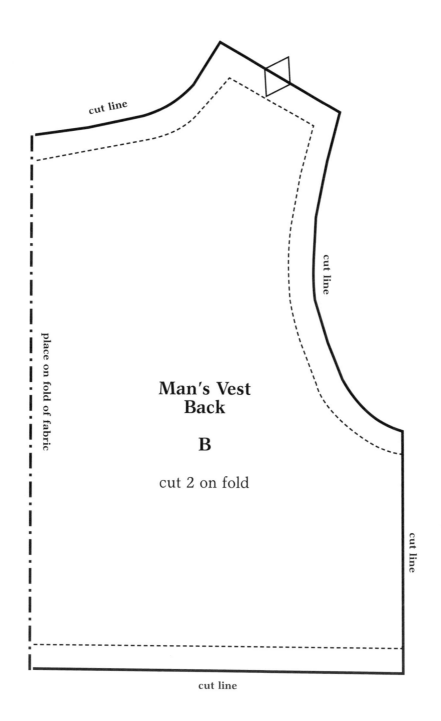

cut line

cut line

place on fold of fabric

**Man's Vest
Back**

B

cut 2 on fold

cut line

cut line

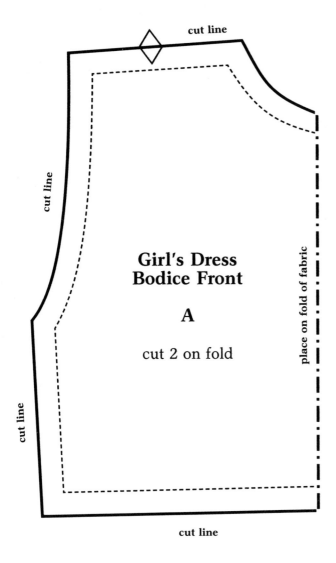

cut line

cut line

cut line

place on fold of fabric

**Girl's Dress
Bodice Front**

A

cut 2 on fold

cut line

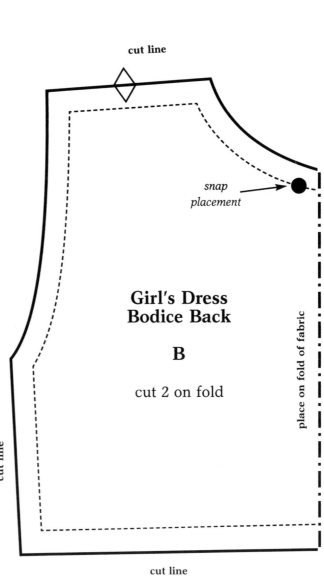

cut line

*snap
placement*

cut line

place on fold of fabric

**Girl's Dress
Bodice Back**

B

cut 2 on fold

cut line

93

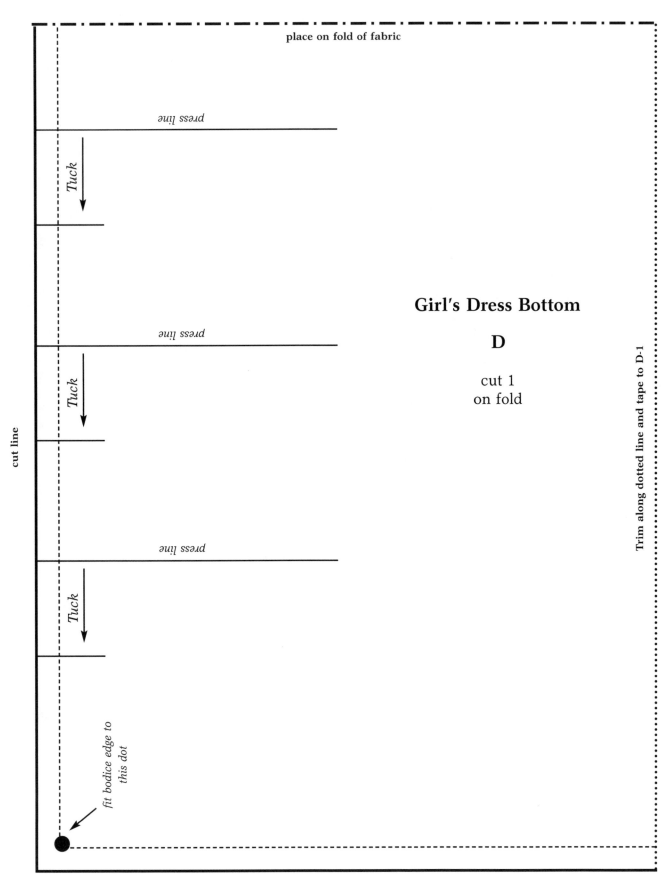

place on fold of fabric

cut line

press line

Tuck

Girl's Dress Bottom

D

cut 1
on fold

press line

Tuck

Trim along dotted line and tape to D-1

press line

Tuck

fit bodice edge to
this dot

cut line

95

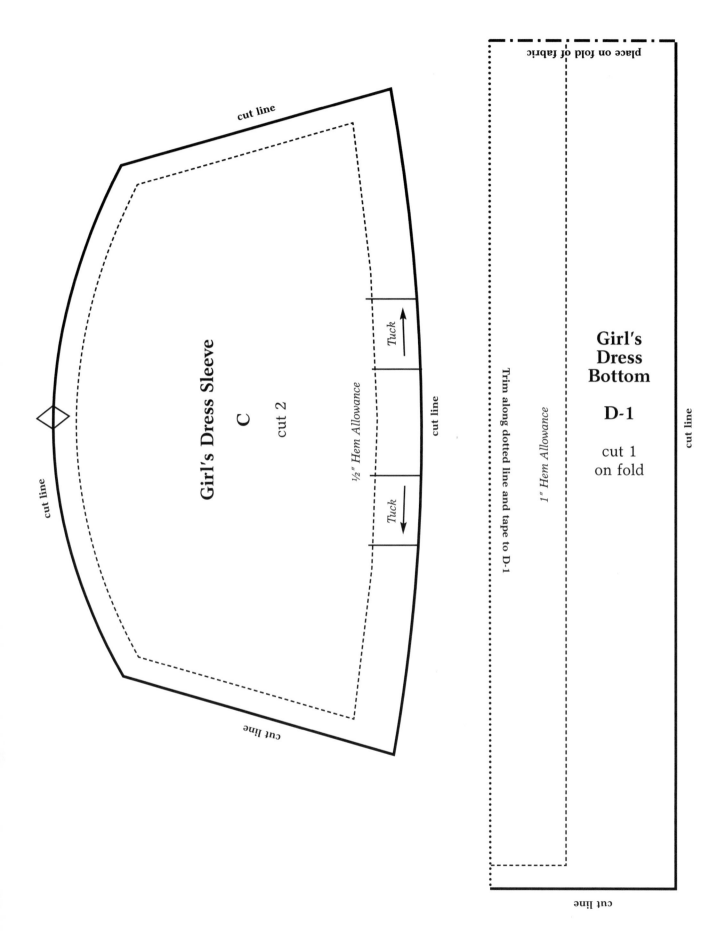

cut line

cut line

cut line

Girl's Dress Sleeve

C

cut 2

½" Hem Allowance

Tuck

Tuck

cut line

cut line

place on fold of fabric

**Girl's
Dress
Bottom**

D-1

cut 1
on fold

Trim along dotted line and tape to D-1

1" Hem Allowance

cut line

cut line

97

cut line

place on fold of fabric

Girl's Apron

A

cut 1
on fold

cut line

1" Hem Allowance

cut line

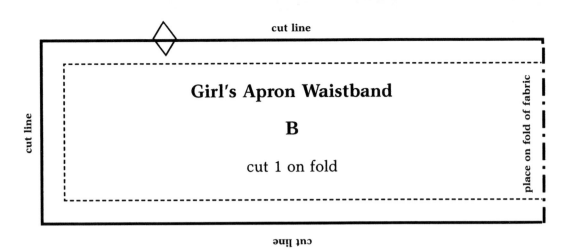

cut line

cut line

Girl's Apron Waistband

B

cut 1 on fold

place on fold of fabric

cut line

cut line

Girl's Pinafore Apron Sleeve Band

B

cut 2

cut line

cut line

cut line

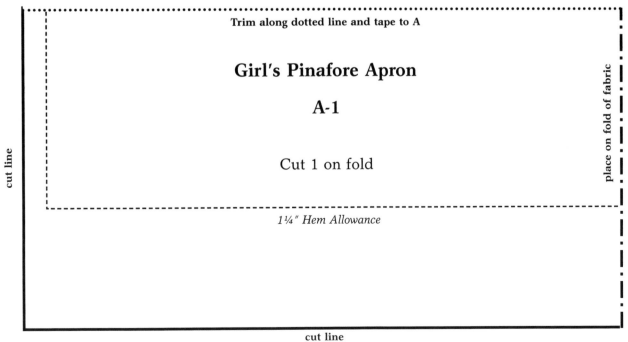

Trim along dotted line and tape to A

Girl's Pinafore Apron

A-1

Cut 1 on fold

place on fold of fabric

cut line

1¼" Hem Allowance

cut line

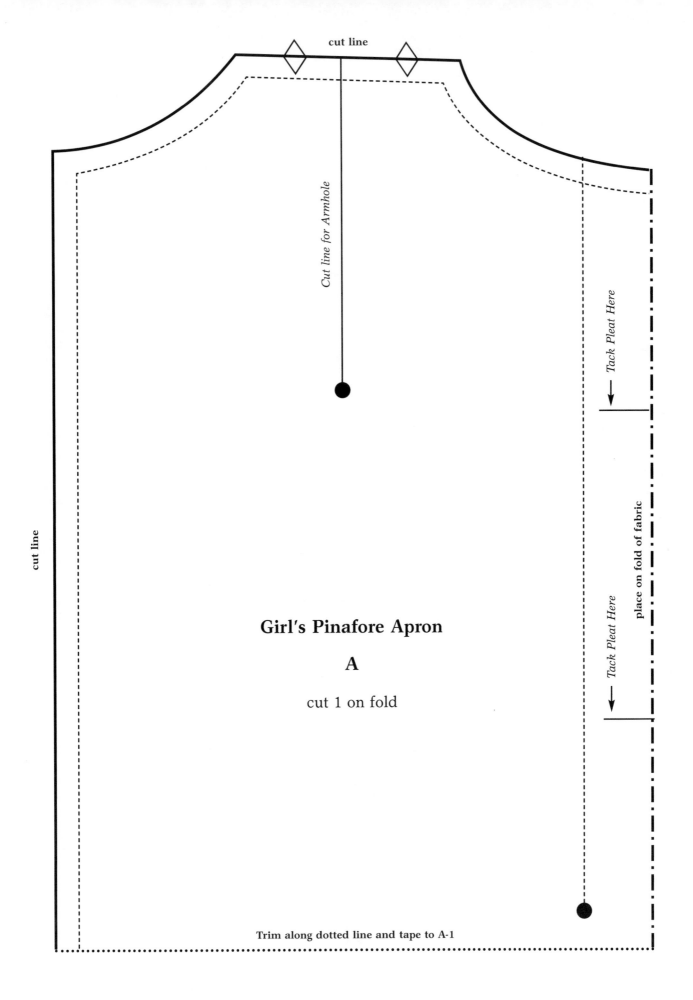

cut line

Girl's Pinafore Apron

A

cut 1 on fold

Cut line for Armhole

Tack Pleat Here

Tack Pleat Here

place on fold of fabric

cut line

Trim along dotted line and tape to A-1

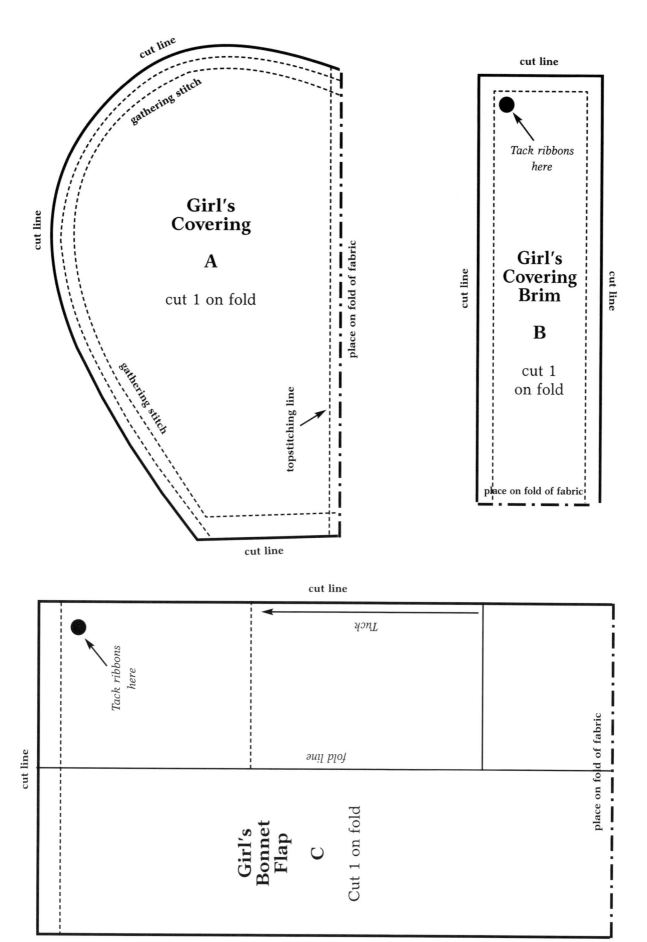

Girl's Covering

A

cut 1 on fold

cut line

gathering stitch

cut line

gathering stitch

topstitching line

place on fold of fabric

cut line

Girl's Covering Brim

B

cut 1 on fold

cut line

Tack ribbons here

cut line

cut line

place on fold of fabric

cut line

Tack ribbons here

Tuck

fold line

Girl's Bonnet Flap

C

Cut 1 on fold

cut line

cut line

place on fold of fabric

cut line

105

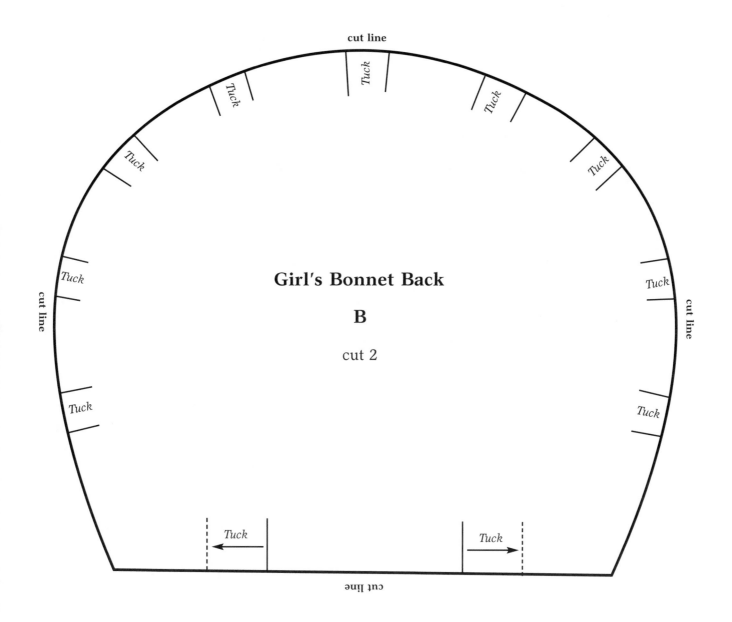

cut line

Tuck

Tuck

Tuck

Tuck

Tuck

Tuck

cut line

Tuck

Tuck

Tuck

Tuck

Girl's Bonnet Back

B

cut 2

Tuck

Tuck

cut line

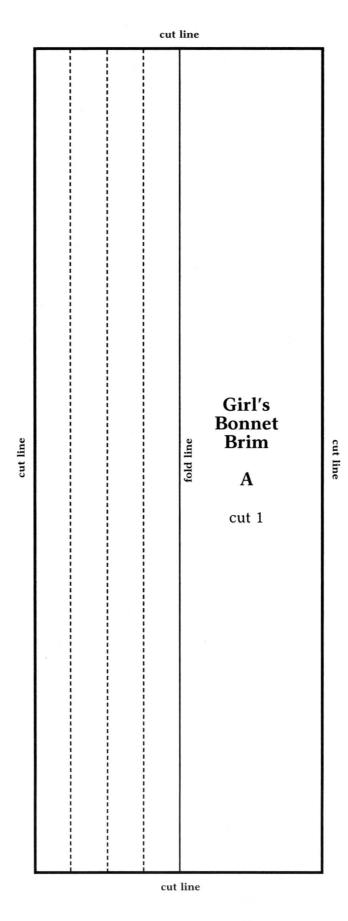

cut line

cut line

cut line

cut line

fold line

**Girl's
Bonnet
Brim**

A

cut 1

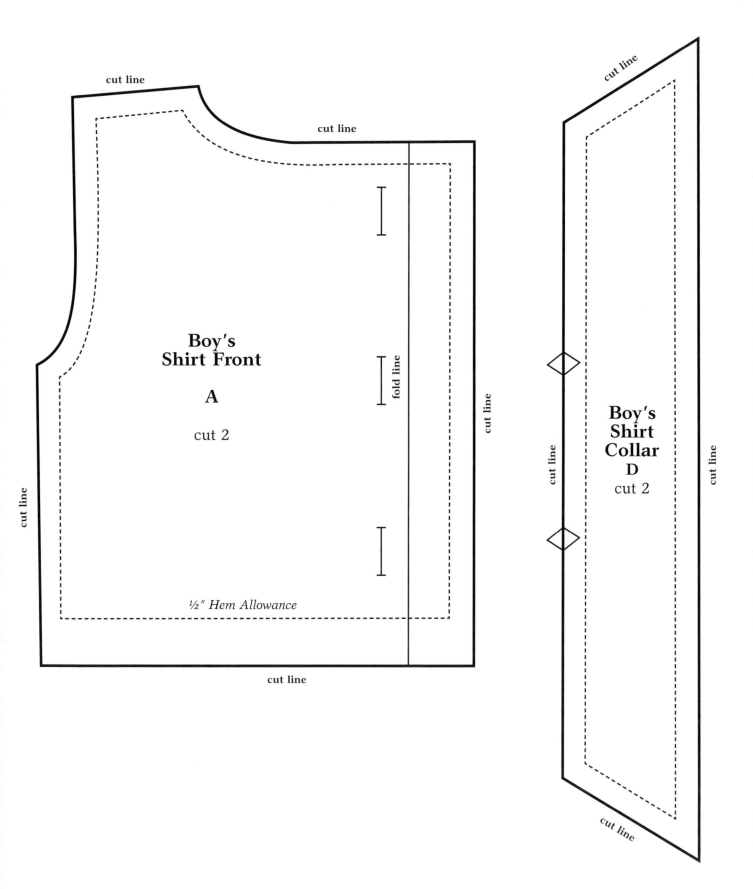

cut line

cut line

cut line

**Boy's
Shirt Front**

A

cut 2

fold line

cut line

½" Hem Allowance

cut line

cut line

cut line

**Boy's
Shirt
Collar
D**
cut 2

cut line

cut line

cut line

111

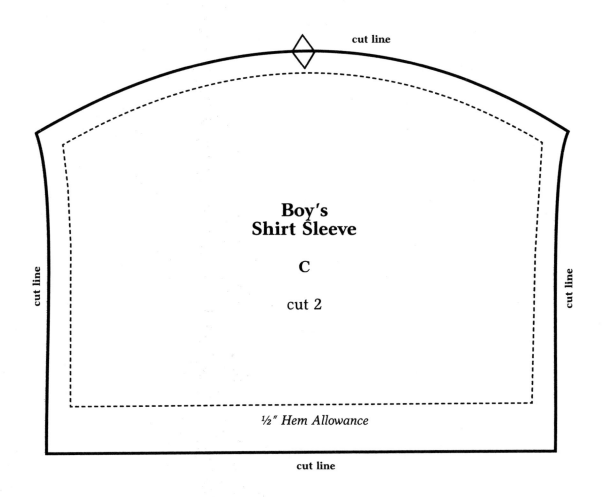

cut line

Boy's Shirt Sleeve

C

cut 2

½" Hem Allowance

cut line

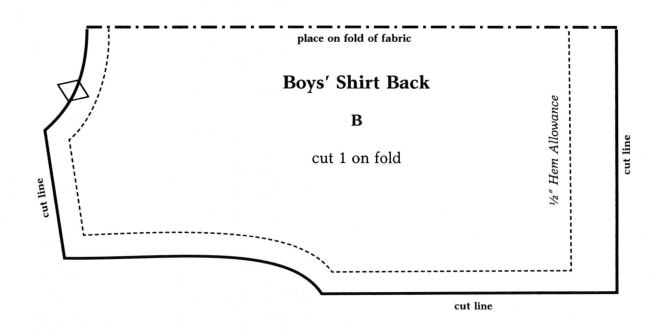

place on fold of fabric

Boys' Shirt Back

B

cut 1 on fold

½" Hem Allowance

cut line

cut line

113

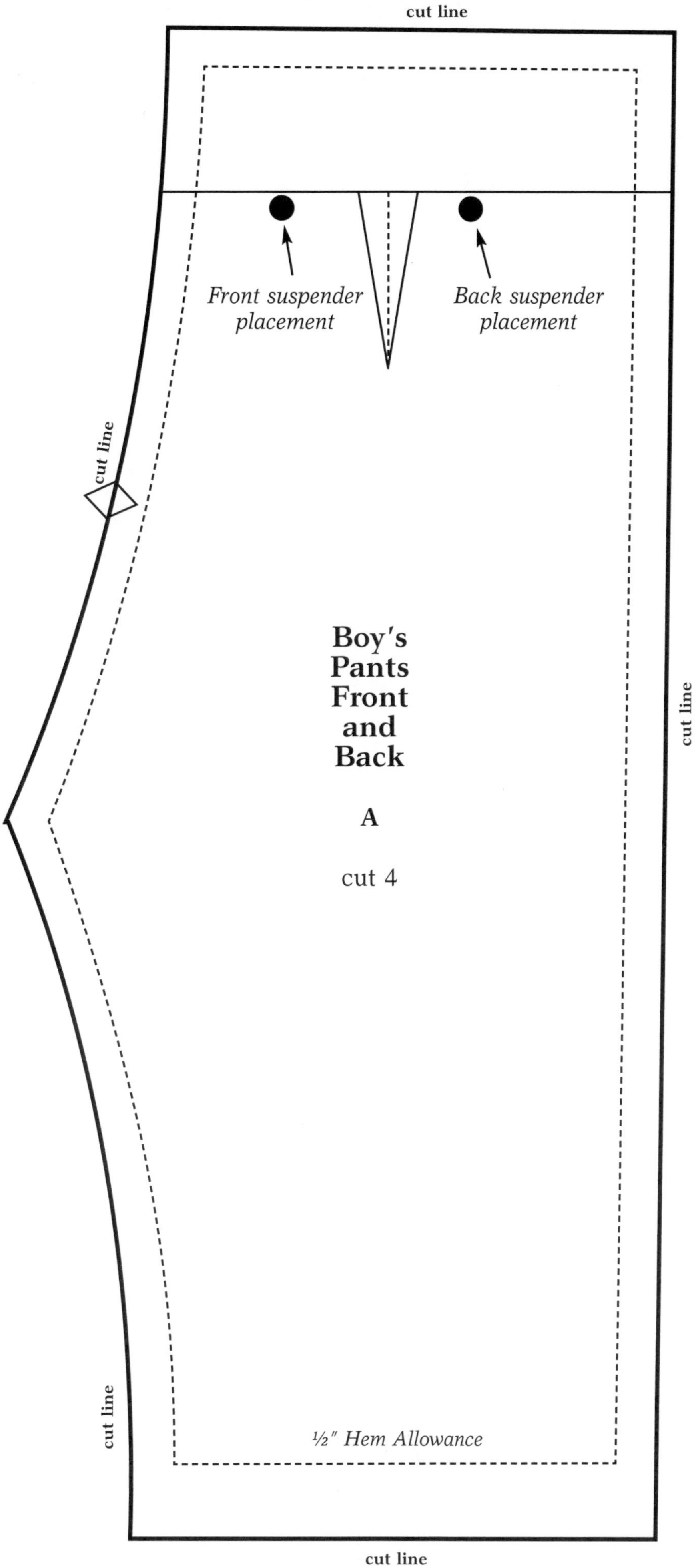

cut line

Front suspender
placement

Back suspender
placement

cut line

**Boy's
Pants
Front
and
Back**

A

cut 4

cut line

cut line

½" Hem Allowance

cut line

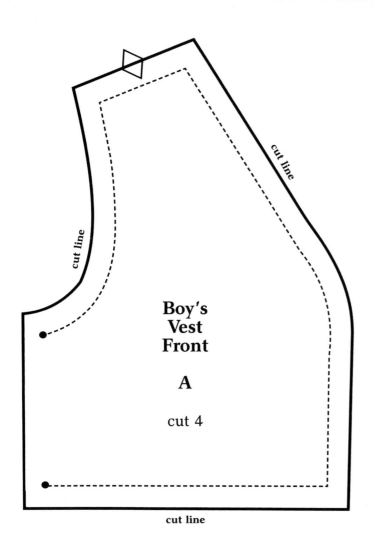

Boy's Vest Front

A

cut 4

cut line

cut line

cut line

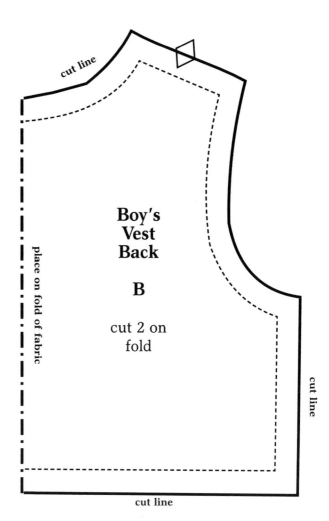

cut line

Boy's Vest Back

B

cut 2 on fold

place on fold of fabric

cut line

cut line

117

Readings and Sources

About the Amish

Budget, The. Sugarcreek, Ohio, 1890. A weekly newspaper serving the Amish and Mennonite communities.

Devoted Christian's Prayer Book. Pathway Publishing House, Aylmer, Ontario, 1967.

Family Life. Amish periodical published monthly. Pathway Publishing House, Aylmer, Ontario.

Good, Merle. **An Amish Portrait: Song of a People.** Good Books, Intercourse, Pennsylvania, 1993.

Good, Merle. **Amos and Susie; An Amish Story.** Good Books, Intercourse, Pennsylvania, 1993.

Good, Merle. **Reuben and the Blizzard.** Good Books, Intercourse, Pennsylvania, 1995.

Good, Merle. **Reuben and the Fire.** Good Books, Intercourse, Pennsylvania, 1993.

Good, Merle. **Reuben and the Quilt.** Good Books, Intercourse, Pennsylvania, 1999.

Good, Merle. **Who Are the Amish?** Good Books, Intercourse, Pennsylvania, 1985.

Good, Merle and Phyllis Good. **20 Most Asked Questions about the Amish and Mennonites.** Good Books, Lancaster, Pennsylvania, 1995.

Good, Phyllis Pellman. **The Best of Amish Cooking.** Good Books, Intercourse, Pennsylvania, 1988.

Good, Phyllis Pellman. **Delicious Amish Recipes.** Good Books, Intercourse, Pennsylvania, 1997.

Good, Phyllis Pellman and Rachel Thomas Pellman. **From Amish and Mennonite Kitchens.** Good Books, Intercourse, Pennsylvania, 1984.

Hostetler, John A. **Amish Life.** Herald Press, Scottdale, Pennsylvania, 1959.

Hostetler, John A. **Amish Society.** Johns Hopkins University Press, Baltimore, Maryland, 1993.

Kaiser, Grace H. **Dr. Frau: A Woman Doctor Among the Amish.** Good Books, Intercourse, Pennsylvania, 1997.

Kraybill, Donald B. **The Puzzles of Amish Life.** Good Books, Intercourse, Pennsylvania, 1998.

Nolt, Steven. **A History of the Amish.** Good Books, Intercourse, Pennsylvania, 1992.

Scott, Stephen. **The Amish Wedding and Other Celebrations of the Old Order Communities.** Good Books, Intercourse, Pennsylvania, 1987.

Scott, Stephen. **Living Without Electricity.** Good Books, Intercourse, Pennsylvania, 1999.

Scott, Stephen. **Why Do They Dress That Way?** Good Books, Intercourse, Pennsylvania, 1986.

Steffy, Jan. **The School Picnic.** Good Books, Intercourse, Pennsylvania, 1987.

Stoltzfus, Louise. **Amish Women.** Good Books, Intercourse, Pennsylvania, 1994.

About Amish Quilts

Bishop, Robert and Elizabeth Safanda. **A Gallery of Amish Quilts.** E. P. Dutton and Company, Inc., New York, New York, 1976.

Gingrich, Ruth Ann and Jan Steffy Mast. **An Amish Nativity.** Good Books, Intercourse, Pennsylvania, 1998.

Granick, Eve Wheatcroft. **The Amish Quilt.** Good Books, Intercourse, Pennsylvania, 1989.

Haders, Phyllis. **Sunshine and Shadow: The Amish and Their Quilts.** Universe Books, New York, New York, 1976.

Horton, Roberta. **Amish Adventure.** C & T Publishing, Lafayette, California, 1983.

Lawson, Suzy. **Amish Inspirations.** Amity Publications, Cottage Grove, Oregon, 1982.

Pellman, Rachel T. **Small Amish Quilt Patterns.** Good Books, Intercourse, Pennsylvania, 1998.

Pellman, Rachel T. and Joanne Ranck. **Quilts Among the Plain People.** Good Books, Intercourse, Pennsylvania, 1981.

Pellman, Rachel and Kenneth. **Amish Doll Quilts, Dolls, and Other Playthings.** Good Books, Intercourse, Pennsylvania, 1986.

Pellman, Rachel and Kenneth. **A Treasury of Amish Quilts.** Good Books, Intercourse, Pennsylvania, 1990.

Pellman, Rachel and Kenneth. **The World of Amish Quilts.** Good Books, Intercourse, Pennsylvania, 1998.

Pottinger, David. **Quilts from the Indiana Amish.** E. P. Dutton, Inc., New York, New York, 1983.

About Other Quilts

Pellman, Rachel T. **Tips for Quilters.** Good Books, Intercourse, Pennsylvania, 1993.

About the Author

Jan Steffy Mast is an expert seamstress and designer. She is the co-author of ***An Amish Nativity, Complete Projects and Instructions,*** and ***Lancaster County Cookbook,*** and author of the children's book, ***The School Picnic,*** set among the Amish. Jan is manager of The People's Place, a heritage interpretation center about the Amish and Mennonites in the village of Intercourse, Pennsylvania, located in the heart of the Old Order Amish settlement.

Jan has developed a close acquaintance with Amish dolls in recent years—because of her three young daughters. They spend two days each week with an Amish family while Jan and her husband Dean are both at work away from their home near Lancaster, Pennsylvania. The girls have discovered the pleasure of playing with Amish dolls.